GORDON RAMSAY'S
fastFOOD

RECIPES FROM THE f WORD

GORDON RAMSAY'S
*fast*FOOD

RECIPES FROM THE f WORD

with Mark Sargeant
and Emily Quah

photographs by Jill Mead

QUADRILLE

NOTES

All spoon measures are level unless otherwise stated:
1 tsp = 5ml spoon; 1 tbsp = 15ml spoon.

All herbs are fresh, and all pepper is freshly ground black pepper
unless otherwise suggested.

I recommend using free-range eggs. If you are pregnant
or in a vulnerable health group, avoid those
recipes that contain raw egg whites
or lightly cooked eggs.

My timings are provided as
guidelines, with a description
of colour or texture where
appropriate. Oven timings apply
to fan-assisted ovens. If using
a conventional oven, increase
the temperature by 15°C (1 Gas Mark).
Use an oven thermometer to check
the accuracy of your oven.

CONTENTS

RECIPE LIST

Beetroot, goat's cheese & apple salad (p65)

Penne, runner beans & goat's cheese (p127)

Bacon, pea & goat's cheese omelette (p93)

Poached duck egg with anchovy fingers (p94)

Scrambled eggs with crabmeat & chives (p95)

Baked egg florentine (p96)

Warm black pudding & quail's egg salad (p99)

Vegetables & grains

Quick minestrone (p156)

Pea & mint soup with Parma ham (p17)

Avocado & cucumber soup (p179)

Artichokes in herb & lemon dressing (p50)

Sicilian caponata (p31)

Caramelised shallot & mushroom toasts (p33)

Roasted vegetable panini (p81)

Salad of griddled asparagus & spinach (p63)

Italian leafy salad with walnut dressing (p66)

Tangerine, frisée & sweet potato salad (p69)

Green bean, red onion & pecorino salad (p104)

Mixed tomato salad (p180)

Grilled aubergine with tahini dressing (p41)

Linguine with tomatoes, olives & capers (p124)

Gratin of roasted peppers, basil & feta (p155)

Easy vegetable curry (p159)

Ratatouille (p161)

Tomato & pesto tart (p103)

Mixed vegetable stir-fry (p203)

Crunchy broccoli & cauliflower gratin (p203)

Wilted spinach with mustard seeds (p197)

Chinese greens with shiitake mushrooms (p210)

Mushy peas (p89)

Sautéed potatoes with panch phora (p204)

Champ (p165)

Chunky chips (p89)

Spicy fried rice with spring onions (p205)

Couscous, broad beans, peas & pancetta (p201)

Nutty bulgar wheat with herbs (p156)

Fruit

Yam pak salad (p209)

Berry & Champagne soup (p221)

Melon with tequila & lime (p120)

Fragrant orange slices (p45)

Lychees with mint sugar (p213)

Blueberries with honey, almonds & yogurt (p26)

Macerated summer berries with clotted cream (p107)

Cherries with almonds & mint (p218)

Figs & blackberries poached in red wine (p219)

Caramelised banana split (p166)

Griddled pineapple with mint & toasted coconut (p198)

Pain perdu with raspberries & ricotta (p215)

Mango fool (p217)

Spiced pan-roasted apples & pears (p58)

Roasted nectarines with amaretti cream (p183)

Banana mousse with butterscotch ripple (p229)

Strawberry shortbreads (p90)

Summer fruit trifles (p233)

No-bake berry cheesecake (p134)

Baked ricotta with caramelised peaches (p235)

Crunchy gooseberry crumble (p226)

Fresh lemonade (p107)

Minty mojito (p245)

Blueberry & pomegranate fizz (p245)

Chocolate & coffee

White chocolate & cherry mousse (p231)

Chocolate fondant (p232)

Easy tiramisu (p77)

INTRODUCTION

When I launched my Sunday lunch campaign last year, 'lack of time' was the excuse most people gave for not cooking. Sadly, ready meals and take-aways have become the staple for many of us. It's tempting and all too easy to blame a hectic lifestyle for eating poorly, but it only takes a bit of effort and organisation to make quick, healthy, delicious meals at home. Enjoying good food is one of life's basic pleasures and there's no better way to bring a family closer together than through cooking and sharing a good meal.

My campaign this time around is to re-define the concept of fast food and prove that anyone can prepare speedy meals in less time than it takes to get a pizza delivered. I have some suggestions to get you on the right track.

First, always try to use the best, seasonal ingredients and treat them simply. Good quality food doesn't call for complicated cooking techniques or garnishes. Take home-grown strawberries, for example. At their peak, a squeeze of lemon juice is all it takes to enhance their natural sweetness and flavour. Equally, you don't need an elaborate sauce to accompany a beautiful fresh fish – a zesty vinaigrette will suffice. As far as meat is concerned, fast food means cooking at high temperatures, so you need to know which cuts are best suited to intense heat.

It is also essential to have a well stocked storecupboard. When it comes to easy weeknight suppers, I recognise that convenience foods such as canned tomatoes, ready roasted peppers and canned beans are useful. Even having basic items to hand in the fridge and freezer can be a time-saver. At a moment's notice, you can whip up an amazing soup using a bag of frozen peas, crème fraîche and leftover pancetta.

Once again, I'm giving you menu ideas, with advice on how to plan your time. The simpler, two-course menus are designed for casual week-night suppers, while the three-course menus are ideal for entertaining. I know what it's like to live life in the fast lane, believe me! However pressed for time you are, please don't neglect what you eat.

Gordon Ramsay.

STORECUPBOARD

A well stocked storecupboard is essential to fast cooking.
If you already have most of the ingredients you need to
hand, it is easy to pick up a few fresh items – on the way
home from work, perhaps. I always have the following
basics in my kitchen:

Oils
Pure olive for cooking, extra virgin olive for drizzling, groundnut for deep-frying, plus other oils for flavouring such as sesame, walnut and truffle-infused olive oil

Vinegars
White and red wine vinegar, aged balsamic, cider, sherry and malt vinegars

Sauces and flavourings
Worcestershire, Tabasco, mustards (wholegrain, English and Dijon) and ketchup

Asian ingredients
Light and dark soy sauce, oyster sauce, sweet chilli sauce, tamarind paste, fish sauce and mirin (rice wine), canned coconut milk

Mediterranean basics
Anchovies in oil, black and green olives, capers, green peppercorns in brine and canned tomatoes

Pasta, grains and noodles
Selection of dried pasta (eg spaghetti, penne and fusilli), rice (jasmine and basmati), couscous, bulgar wheat and rice noodles

Canned pulses
Butter beans, chickpeas, flageolet and mixed beans

Preserved vegetables in jars
Artichoke hearts, ready-roasted peppers, sun-dried tomatoes in oil, pickles and gherkins

Baking essentials
Flours (plain and self-raising), sugars (caster, granulated, icing, light brown and Demerara), cocoa powder and vanilla extract

Sweet extras
Amaretti biscuits, runny honey, good quality dark chocolate (about 70% cocoa solids), white chocolate, desiccated coconut and sponge fingers (savoiardi)

Fresh standbys

I use the following ingredients so frequently that I always make sure I have them in the kitchen. Having a regular stock of these foods certainly helps to produce good fast meals. Add them to your weekly shopping list whenever you're about to run out:

Vegetable rack:
- potatoes
- red and white onions
- regular or banana shallots
- garlic
- ginger

Fridge:
- butter
- milk
- Greek yogurt
- crème fraîche
- double cream
- Parmesan or pecorino cheese
- goat's cheese
- cream cheese or mascarpone
- free-range eggs
- pancetta (slices or cubetti) or smoked bacon
- lemons and limes
- fresh herbs (see right)

Freezer:
- bread (country loaves, rolls, sliced white or brown bread, pita bread)
- broad beans and peas
- fresh stocks (chicken, fish and vegetable)
- puff pastry
- good quality ice cream (including vanilla)

Other essentials

Seasonings

To take away seasoning from a chef is like sending a soldier out to war unarmed. Needless to say, a good sea salt (such as Maldon or Fleur de Sel) and black peppercorns are crucial in my kitchens. I also use green and white peppercorns occasionally. Invest in robust salt and pepper mills and freshly grind sea salt and pepper as required.

Spices

I also rely on various spices to jazz up sweet and savoury dishes. I recommend that you buy these little and often, as their flavour deteriorates surprisingly quickly. Store them in a cool, dark cupboard. I use the following spices on a regular basis: cardamom pods, celery salt, cinnamon (whole sticks and ground), cloves, coriander seeds, cumin seeds, curry powder, fennel seeds, garam masala, ground ginger, juniper berries, chilli powder, mustard seeds, whole nutmeg for grating, paprika, saffron strands, star anise and vanilla pods.

Herbs

I cannot imagine cooking without fresh herbs to hand. Grow a selection of herbs – a bay tree, rosemary, sage, parsley, mint, chives etc – in the garden if you can. Otherwise keep little pots of growing herbs on the windowsill – even tender basil, flat leaf parsley and coriander will thrive during the warmer months. In winter, buy parsley, thyme and coriander in bunches from a greengrocer or market, rather than in packets from a supermarket if you can.

Spirits, liqueurs and wine

Many a dish is improved with a generous splash of alcohol. In addition to red and white wine, I'd recommend keeping a good bottle of brandy, Cognac or Calvados; Marsala or Madeira; amaretto liqueur and rum; plus a sweet dessert wine, such as Muscat or Vin Santo.

fast 5 soups

Leek, potato & smoked haddock soup
Pea & mint soup with Parma ham
Butter bean, chorizo & red onion soup
Chilled melon soup with crab garnish
Beetroot soup with smoked duck

Leek, potato & smoked haddock soup

Serves 4

3 tbsp olive oil, plus extra to drizzle
2 large leeks, trimmed and thinly sliced
500g Charlotte potatoes, peeled and cut
   into 1cm cubes
1 tsp curry powder
sea salt and black pepper
400ml milk (whole or semi-skimmed)
300ml fish or vegetable stock
1 bay leaf
250g smoked haddock fillets
knob of butter
small bunch of chives, finely chopped

Heat the olive oil in a large pan and sauté the leeks, potatoes, curry powder and seasoning over medium heat for 5 minutes or until the leeks have softened. Add the milk, stock and bay leaf, bring to the boil, then simmer for 5 minutes until the potatoes are tender.

Add the fish and poach for 2–3 minutes until flaky. Lift out with a slotted spoon and break into large flakes, removing the skin. Transfer a quarter of the leeks and potatoes to a bowl, add the butter and crush lightly with a fork. Stir through the haddock and chives.

Discard the bay leaf and whiz the soup with a blender until smooth and creamy. Check the seasoning and reheat, adding a little extra hot stock or water to thin if needed. Pile the crushed potato and haddock mixture in the centre of warm bowls and pour the soup around. Drizzle with a little olive oil and serve.

Pea & mint soup with Parma ham

2 tbsp olive oil, plus extra to drizzle
4 slices of Parma ham, chopped
sea salt and black pepper
large handful of mint (about 6 sprigs),
   leaves only
500g peas (fresh or frozen)
200g crème fraîche

Heat the olive oil in a frying pan. Sprinkle the Parma ham with black pepper and fry over a high heat until golden brown and crisp, turning once. Drain in a colander, then on kitchen paper to remove all excess oil.

Add the mint leaves to a medium saucepan of boiling salted water. Bring back to the boil, then add the peas and blanch for 2–3 minutes until they are just tender and still bright green. Drain, reserving the liquor.

Tip the peas and mint into a blender. Add just enough of the hot liquor (about 500ml) to cover and whiz to a smooth purée. Add a generous drizzle of olive oil and all but 4 tbsp crème fraîche. Season with salt and pepper to taste and pulse for a few seconds to combine.

Pour the soup into warm bowls and dollop the reserved crème fraîche on top. Scatter over the crispy Parma ham and serve.

Butter bean, chorizo & red onion soup

Serves 4

225g chorizo sausage, skin removed

3 tbsp olive oil, plus extra to drizzle

2 red onions, peeled and finely chopped

2 garlic cloves, peeled and very finely
  sliced

few thyme sprigs

2 x 420g cans butter beans, drained and
  rinsed

sea salt and black pepper

squeeze of lemon juice

large handful of flat leaf parsley,
  roughly chopped

Chop the chorizo into small bite-sized pieces. Put the kettle on to boil.

Heat the olive oil in a heavy-based saucepan and add the onions, garlic and thyme. Cook, stirring, for 2 minutes then add the chorizo. Stir over a high heat for a few minutes until the oil has taken on a reddish-golden hue from the chorizo.

Tip in the butter beans and pour in just enough boiling water to cover them. Bring to a simmer and cook gently for about 10 minutes.

Season generously with salt and pepper and add a squeeze of lemon juice. Scatter over the chopped parsley and ladle the soup into warm bowls to serve.

Chilled melon soup with crab garnish

Serves 4

2 charentais (or cantaloupe) melons, chilled
4 tbsp natural yogurt

CRAB GARNISH:
150g white crabmeat
½ shallot, peeled and finely chopped
½ crisp apple (eg Granny Smith), peeled and finely diced
few coriander leaves, chopped, plus extra to garnish
1 tbsp wholegrain mustard
2–3 tbsp mayonnaise
squeeze of lime juice
sea salt and black pepper

Halve the melons, deseed and peel, then cut into chunks. Tip into a blender and add the yogurt, 6–7 ice cubes and a tiny pinch of salt. Whiz to a very smooth purée. Pour into a bowl and place in the freezer to chill while you prepare the crab.

Put the crabmeat into a bowl and run your fingers through it to pick out any bits of shell. Add the shallot, apple and chopped coriander, then stir in the mustard and enough mayonnaise to bind the mixture together. Add lime juice and season with salt and pepper to taste.

To serve, place a large dollop of crabmeat in the centre of each chilled soup bowl. Pour the cold melon soup around and garnish with a few coriander leaves.

Beetroot soup with smoked duck

Serves 4

3–4 tbsp olive oil, plus extra to drizzle
1 onion, peeled and chopped
1 bay leaf
2 garlic cloves, peeled and crushed
2 large carrots, peeled and chopped
1 celery stalk, trimmed and chopped
2 x 250g packs ready-cooked beetroot
   in natural juices
600ml hot vegetable or chicken stock
sea salt and black pepper
squeeze of lemon juice
200g smoked duck breasts, thinly sliced
soured cream, to drizzle

Heat a large saucepan and pour in the olive oil. Add the onion, bay leaf, garlic, carrots and celery. Cook over high heat, stirring often, for 4–5 minutes until the vegetables begin to soften.

Meanwhile, coarsely grate the beetroot (wearing rubber gloves to prevent your hands from staining). Add to the pan and pour in the stock. Cover and simmer for 10 minutes until the vegetables are tender. Discard the bay leaf.

Whiz the soup to a smooth purée using a hand-held (or free-standing) blender. Taste and adjust the seasoning with salt, pepper and lemon juice. Reheat gently if necessary.

Ladle the soup into warm bowls. Lay the smoked duck slices on top and drizzle over the soured cream and olive oil to serve.

Light & healthy
{everyday menu}

I think of this menu as the ideal ladies' lunch – light, flavourful and full of healthy superfoods. If you want a more substantial meal, serve the fish with some crushed new potatoes. Otherwise, keep it light and finish with a creamy, but guilt-free, blueberry dessert. Serves 4.

planning your menu

Pan-fried hake with tomato relish
Blueberries with honey, almonds & yogurt

- Combine the yogurt, honey and blueberries. Divide among serving bowls and chill.
- Toast the almonds and cool.
- Prepare the ingredients for the tomato relish.
- Fry the fish and make the relish.
- Serve the main course.
- Top the dessert with toasted almonds and serve.

PAN-FRIED HAKE WITH TOMATO RELISH

66 Hake is an under-rated fish, which is a shame because it has a subtle and delicious flavour, similar to cod. Best of all, it is environmentally sustainable, yet inexpensive. It is also easy to prepare as it has relatively few bones. 99

Serves 4
4 hake fillets, about 175g each
sea salt and black pepper
3 tbsp olive oil, plus extra to drizzle
250g vine-ripened cherry or small plum
   tomatoes, quartered
bunch of spring onions (about 8),
   trimmed and chopped
1 tsp caster sugar
splash of white wine vinegar
few thyme sprigs (leaves only)
small handful of coriander leaves, chopped

TIP Heating the fish fillets slowly in a cold pan prevents them from curling up during frying. This works really well for firm fish with thin skins, such as hake.

Check the hake fillets for any pin bones, removing any you find with a pair of tweezers. Season the fish with salt and pepper. Put 2 tbsp olive oil in a cold frying pan and lay the fish fillets on top, skin side down.

Slowly warm the pan over a low heat, then increase the heat to medium after a minute or two. Fry until the skin is golden and crisp, and the fillets are cooked two-thirds of the way through.

Turn the fish over and cook the flesh side for 50–60 seconds only. Transfer to a plate lined with kitchen paper to drain; keep warm.

Add 1 tbsp olive oil to the pan and sauté the tomatoes and spring onions for a minute. Add the sugar and a splash of wine vinegar. Cook over a high heat for a minute or two until the vinegar has cooked off and the tomatoes are a little soft but still retaining their shape.

Season the tomatoes well, toss in the herbs and divide among four warm plates. Place the hake fillets, skin side up, on top and serve immediately.

BLUEBERRIES WITH HONEY, ALMONDS & YOGURT

"We always have berries and yogurt in the fridge so I think of this as a speedy storecupboard dessert, which is also great for breakfast. Toast the almonds rather than buy them ready-toasted – it only takes a minute and the flavour is much better."

Serves 4
4 tbsp flaked almonds
150ml Greek yogurt
2 tbsp runny honey
250g blueberries

Toss the flaked almonds in a small,
dry frying pan over a medium-high heat until fragrant and golden brown. (Don't leave them unattended as they catch and burn easily). Tip into a bowl and leave to cool.

Mix the yogurt and honey together
in a bowl and fold in the blueberries. Divide among small bowls and chill until ready to serve.

Scatter the toasted almonds over
the dessert and drizzle with a little more honey if you like, to serve.

"Great fast food depends on using top quality ingredients. Finding a good butcher, fishmonger and farmers' market or greengrocer is the key."

*f*ast **starters**

Sicilian caponata
Caramelised shallot & mushroom toasts
Sautéed scallops with sweetcorn salsa
Salmon ceviche
Soused herrings with curry cream

Sicilian caponata

Serves 4

5 tbsp olive oil
1 aubergine, trimmed and cut into chunks
1 onion, peeled and chopped
2 celery stalks, trimmed and chopped
1 red pepper, deseeded and chopped
sea salt and black pepper
5 large tomatoes
2 garlic cloves, peeled and chopped
2 tbsp caster sugar
1–1½ tbsp red wine or balsamic vinegar
100g green olives, pitted and sliced
50g capers, rinsed and drained
handful of basil leaves, torn
50g toasted pine nuts

Heat the olive oil in a wide, heavy-based pan and sauté the aubergine, onion, celery and red pepper with some seasoning over a high heat for about 5 minutes.

Drop the tomatoes into a pot of boiling water for a minute, refresh under cold water and peel. Halve, deseed and cut into chunks. Add to the pan with the garlic, sugar, vinegar, olives and capers.

Cook over a high heat for 5–8 minutes, stirring occasionally, until the aubergine is tender. Check the seasoning and leave to cool slightly (or to room temperature).

Scatter the torn basil and toasted pine nuts over the caponata and serve with toasted country bread.

Caramelised shallot & mushroom toasts

Serves 4

6 banana shallots (or 12 regular ones), peeled and thinly sliced
2 tbsp olive oil, plus extra to drizzle
few thyme sprigs, leaves only
1 garlic clove (unpeeled), smashed
sea salt and black pepper
1 tsp caster sugar
400g portabellini (or sliced portabello) mushrooms
few knobs of butter
splash of sherry vinegar
handful of flat leaf parsley, chopped
4 thick slices of rustic white bread

Sauté the shallots in a pan over a medium heat with the olive oil, thyme, garlic and seasoning for 3–4 minutes until starting to soften. Add the sugar and increase the heat to high. Stir and cook for a few more minutes until the shallots are lightly caramelised.

Add the mushrooms and butter. Fry for a couple of minutes until lightly browned, then splash in the sherry vinegar and add a little more seasoning. Cook for a minute or two until the liquid has evaporated. Discard the garlic. Toss in the chopped parsley.

Toast the bread and place a slice on each warm plate. Spoon the shallots and mushrooms on top and drizzle with a little more olive oil to serve, if you like.

Sautéed scallops with sweetcorn salsa

Serves 4

12 scallops, shelled and cleaned
½ tsp medium curry powder
2 tbsp olive oil
small handful of rocket leaves

SWEETCORN SALSA:
400g can sweetcorn, drained
200g cherry tomatoes, quartered
1 red chilli, deseeded and finely chopped
1 red onion, peeled and finely chopped
2 spring onions, trimmed and finely sliced
3 tbsp sesame oil
handful of coriander, roughly chopped
juice of 2 limes
dash of light soy sauce
sea salt and black pepper

For the salsa, combine all the ingredients in a saucepan and stir over a medium heat for 2 minutes to warm through.

Halve the scallops horizontally into two discs. Mix the curry powder with 1 tsp sea salt and sprinkle over the scallops. Heat a large frying pan over a high heat and add the olive oil. Pan-fry the scallops for 1 minute each side until golden brown at the edges, turning them in the same order you put them in the pan to ensure they cook evenly; don't overcook.

Spoon the salsa on to warm plates and arrange the scallops on top. Scatter over a few rocket leaves and serve.

Salmon ceviche

Serves 4

300g very fresh salmon fillet, skinned
1 red chilli, deseeded and thinly sliced
1 spring onion, trimmed and thinly sliced
  on the diagonal
1 fat garlic clove, peeled and thinly sliced
small handful of coriander leaves,
  shredded
small handful of mixed cress (optional)

DRESSING:
juice of 1 lemon
2 tbsp light soy sauce
2 tbsp sesame oil
drizzle of olive oil
sea salt and black pepper
pinch of caster sugar

For the dressing, whisk the lemon juice, soy, sesame and olive oils together in a bowl. Season with salt and pepper, and add a little sugar to taste.

Slice the salmon and arrange on serving plates, overlapping the slices very slightly. Scatter over the red chilli, spring onion and garlic. Spoon over the dressing and leave to marinate for 5–10 minutes.

Scatter the coriander over the ceviche when you are ready to serve and garnish with mixed cress, if you like.

Soused herrings with curry cream

Serves 4

4 x 270g jars rollmops with onions

150ml crème fraîche

1–2 tbsp no-cook Gujarat Masala curry
  paste

sea salt and black pepper

4 handfuls of mixed salad leaves (rocket,
  oak leaf, frisée etc)

1 lemon, quartered

Drain the rollmops
and open out the herrings, separating the fillets from the onions. Arrange two rows of onion on each serving plate and lay the herring fillets, skin side up, on top.

Mix the crème fraîche
and 1 tbsp curry paste together and season with salt and pepper. Taste and add a little more curry paste if you prefer more of a kick.

Drizzle the curry cream
over the herring fillets. Arrange a pile of salad leaves on each plate and serve, with lemon wedges on the side.

A taste of Morocco
{entertaining menu}

Slow-cooked aromatic tagines typify this cuisine, but here I've created a Moroccan-inspired quick menu. Serve warm flat bread with the grilled aubergines, and accompany the bream with couscous. A fragrant orange dessert is the ideal refreshing finish. Serves 4.

planning your menu

Grilled aubergine with tahini dressing
Black bream with chermoula
          + couscous   + mixed salad
Fragrant orange slices

- Prepare oranges, dress with honey and orange blossom water, then chill.
- Griddle the aubergine.
- Make the tahini dressing.
- Prepare the fish and chermoula.
- Put the fish in the oven to bake.
- Prepare the couscous and salad.
- Dress the aubergine with the tahini dressing and serve.
- Serve the fish with the chermoula and accompaniments.
- Scatter the cinnamon and nuts over the oranges and serve.

GRILLED AUBERGINE
WITH TAHINI DRESSING

" I love this simple Moroccan dish. It makes a delicious starter and you can even prepare it a day ahead – just remember to take it out of the fridge 20 minutes before serving as it is best eaten at room temperature. **"**

Serves 4
1 large aubergine, trimmed
olive oil, to brush and drizzle
sea salt and black pepper
few rosemary sprigs, plus extra to garnish
3 bay leaves, plus extra to garnish
juice of ½ lemon

TAHINI DRESSING:
1 tbsp tahini paste
2 tbsp natural yogurt
1 tbsp lemon juice
1 tsp runny honey
1 garlic clove, peeled and finely crushed

TIP This tahini dressing is equally good with grilled lamb and chicken. Make up a double quantity and store in a jar in the fridge; it will keep for a few days.

Cut the aubergine into 1cm thick slices. Generously brush with olive oil on both sides and rub all over with salt and pepper. Toss with the rosemary and bay leaves.

Heat a griddle pan, then add the aubergine slices with the herbs. Griddle for 4–5 minutes on each side until cooked. Transfer to a serving bowl and while still warm, drizzle over some more olive oil and the lemon juice. Toss well to coat and set aside to cool.

For the tahini dressing, mix all the ingredients together in a bowl until smooth. Stir in 1–2 tbsp hot water to loosen the dressing until it is the consistency of thick double cream. Season to taste with salt and pepper.

Drizzle the dressing over the griddled aubergine and garnish with a few fresh bay leaves and rosemary sprigs. Serve some warm flat bread on the side.

BLACK BREAM WITH CHERMOULA

❝ I think of Moroccan chermoula as the spicy equivalent of an Italian gremolata. Both include garlic, lemon juice and olive oil, but chermoula is spiked with the heady fragrance of cumin, coriander and paprika. It can be used as a marinade or simply as a zesty sauce to spoon over fish dishes, such as mouth-watering baked bream. ❞

2 sea bream, about 700g each,
    scaled and gutted
sea salt and black pepper
handful of rosemary sprigs
handful of thyme sprigs
2 lemons, sliced
olive oil, to drizzle

CHERMOULA:
2 tsp cumin seeds
2 tsp coriander seeds
2 garlic cloves, peeled and grated
    or roughly chopped
1 tsp sweet paprika
finely grated zest and juice of ½ lemon
4 tbsp extra virgin olive oil
large handful of coriander leaves,
    roughly chopped

Heat the oven to 220°C/Gas 7. Score the fish on both sides at 2cm intervals and rub with a little salt and pepper. Stuff the cavity of each fish with a sprig each of rosemary and thyme.

Scatter the lemon slices and a few herb sprigs over the base of one large (or two smaller) sturdy roasting tray(s) and drizzle with olive oil. Place the fish on top and scatter over the remaining herbs. Drizzle a little more olive oil over the fish and season again with salt and pepper.

To prepare the chermoula, toast the cumin and coriander seeds in a frying pan over a low heat until they release their fragrance. Tip into a mortar and grind to a powder with the pestle. Add the garlic, paprika, a pinch of salt and a grinding of pepper. Pound to a paste, then stir in the rest of the ingredients, adding the coriander at the end.

Bake the fish in the oven for about 15–20 minutes until it is just cooked through. It's ready when the thickest part of the flesh comes away easily from the bone.

Transfer the bream to a large warm serving platter. Dress the fish with the chermoula as you fillet them to serve.

FRAGRANT ORANGE SLICES

" This simple, refreshing orange salad is often served as a dessert in Morocco, where it is usual to end a meal with fresh fruit and nuts. The orange blossom water enhances the flavour and fragrance. **"**

Serves 4
4 large oranges
1½ tbsp runny honey
1 tbsp orange blossom water
pinch of ground cinnamon
50g toasted walnuts (or pistachios),
**   roughly chopped**

Slice off the top and bottom of each orange and place upright on a chopping board. Following the curve of the fruit, cut off the skin, making sure that you remove the white pith as well. Turn the peeled orange on one side and cut into slices, removing any pips as you do so.

Arrange the orange slices overlapping on individual plates. Mix the honey with the orange blossom water until evenly blended, then drizzle over the orange slices. Mix the cinnamon and chopped walnuts together and scatter over the oranges to serve.

fast antipasti

Balsamic figs with crumbled Roquefort
Bruschetta with tomato & Parma ham
Bresaola with rocket & Parmesan
Marinated mozzarella
Artichokes in herb & lemon dressing

Balsamic figs with crumbled Roquefort

Serves 4

Take 100g Roquefort (or any leftover blue cheese you may have in the fridge) and wrap well in all-purpose cling film. Freeze for at least 10–15 minutes until firm.

Cut 8 ripe figs into quarters and randomly scatter over four serving plates. Unwrap the blue cheese and grate a generous layer over the figs. Drizzle with some good quality balsamic vinegar and extra virgin olive oil. Grind over a little black pepper and serve straight away.

Bruschetta with tomato & Parma ham
Serves 4

Cut 6–8 ripe cherry tomatoes into quarters and put into a bowl. Add a few shredded basil leaves, 1½ tbsp red wine vinegar, 4 tbsp olive oil and some salt and pepper. Give the mixture a stir and set aside.

Toast 4 thick slices of ciabatta, then rub one side with a halved fat garlic clove. Place on serving plates and spoon over the tomato mixture. Drape each bruschetta with 2 slices of Parma ham or prosciutto and serve.

Bresaola with rocket & Parmesan
Serves 4

Arrange 6 slices of bresaola (salt-cured beef) on each serving plate, allowing the sides to overlap a little.

Scatter over a small handful of rocket leaves, then drizzle with some extra virgin olive oil. Sprinkle with freshly grated Parmesan, a little lemon juice and freshly cracked black pepper to serve.

Marinated mozzarella

Thickly slice four 150g fresh buffalo mozzarella balls. Generously drizzle a serving dish or platter with some extra virgin olive oil, then sprinkle with sea salt, black pepper and a handful of torn basil leaves.

Arrange the mozzarella slices in a single layer in the dish. Add another generous drizzle of extra virgin olive oil and scatter over more torn basil leaves, salt and pepper. Squeeze over a little lemon juice.

Cover with cling film and leave to marinate for 10–15 minutes in the fridge (or longer if you have time). Serve slightly chilled.

Artichokes in herb & lemon dressing
Serves 4

Drain a 400g can or jar of good quality artichoke hearts (or ready-prepared artichokes from a deli). Toss with 1 finely chopped garlic clove and a squeeze of lemon juice. Drizzle with extra virgin olive oil and season with salt and pepper to taste. Leave to infuse for at least 10 minutes.

Chop a small handful of chives and flat leaf parsley and stir through the marinated artichokes just before serving.

"A good set of knives enables you to work quickly and efficiently. Keep them sharp – blunt knives are inclined to slip off food into waiting fingers."

Country cooking
{everyday menu}

Full of rustic, autumnal flavours, this is comfort food at its best. Meaty pork chops go well with robust sauces – in this instance, a chunky, tangy, lightly spiced tomato and mushroom sauce. Round off the meal with pan-roasted apples and pears – ideally from your garden or local farmers' market. Serves 4.

Baked pork chops with a piquant sauce
Spiced pan-roasted apples & pears

- **Preheat the oven. Prepare the pork chops ready for baking.**
- **Chop the vegetables for the sauce.**
- **Put the chops in the oven.**
- **Make the mushroom and tomato sauce and leave to simmer.**
- **Prepare the apples and pears, make the spiced caramel and add the fruit.**
- **Remove the pork from the oven and leave to rest.**
- **Add the Calvados and apple juice to the caramelised fruit and reduce.**
- **Serve the pork with the sauce.**
- **Serve the caramelised apples and pears.**

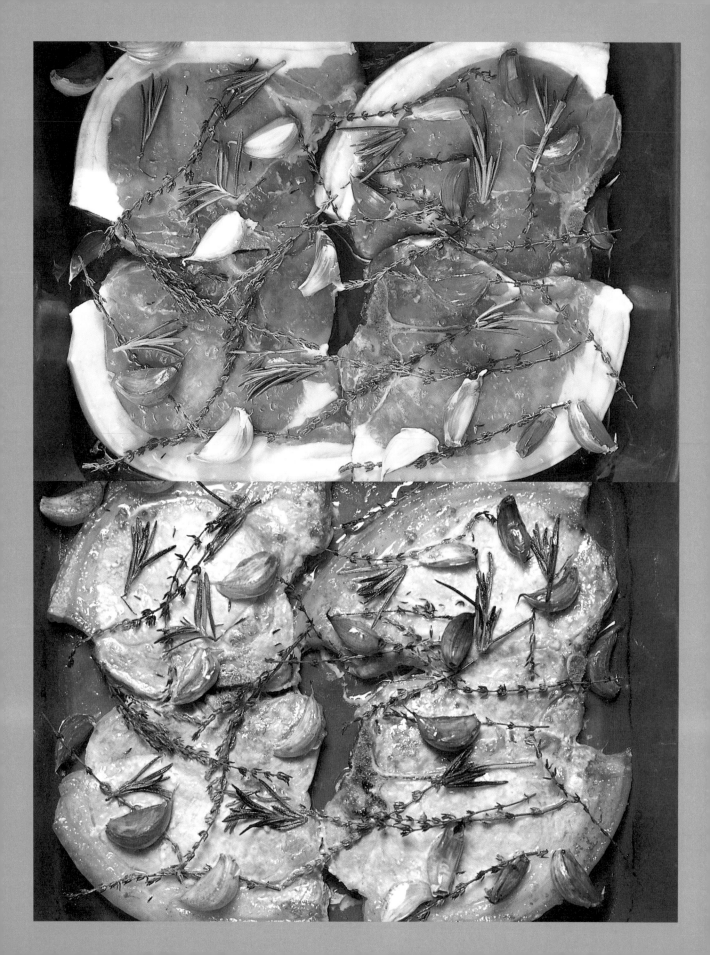

BAKED PORK CHOPS WITH A PIQUANT SAUCE

" These chops are quite satisfying as they are, perhaps with some bread to mop up the sauce, but you could serve them with rice – nutty Camargue red rice would be perfect. The piquant sauce is my adaptation of a rustic Spanish tomato sauce. "

Serves 4
4 pork chops, about 250g each
a little olive oil, plus extra to drizzle
few thyme sprigs
few rosemary sprigs (leaves only)
½ head of garlic, separated into cloves
    (unpeeled)
sea salt and black pepper

SAUCE:
3 tbsp olive oil
1 large onion, peeled and finely chopped
1 red pepper, deseeded and finely chopped
1 red chilli, deseeded and finely chopped
200g chestnut mushrooms, trimmed and
    finely sliced
400g can chopped tomatoes
sea salt and black pepper
1 tsp caster sugar

Heat the oven to 200°C/Gas 6. Place the pork chops in a large, lightly oiled baking dish and scatter over the thyme sprigs, rosemary leaves, garlic cloves and salt. Drizzle with a little olive oil and bake for 20 minutes or until the pork chops are cooked through.

Make the sauce in the meantime. Heat the olive oil in a wide pan and add the onion, red pepper, chilli and mushrooms. Stir over a high heat for 3–4 minutes until the vegetables begin to soften. Tip in the tomatoes. Season with salt and pepper and add the sugar and a splash of water. Simmer for 10–12 minutes until the onions are tender and the tomato sauce has thickened. Taste and adjust the seasoning.

Take the chops out of the oven and leave to rest in a warm place for 5 minutes. Then pour any pan juices into the sauce and reheat. Ladle a generous amount of sauce over the chops to serve.

SPICED PAN-ROASTED APPLES & PEARS

"Whole spices lend a unique fragrance and flavour to caramelised apples and pears. If preparing in advance, peel and cut the fruit, then spread out on a clean tea towel to dry out slightly. Don't worry if the pieces discolour a little, as they will be coated in a lovely, dark caramel anyway."

Serves 4
2 firm apples (eg Braeburn)
4 firm pears (eg Conference)
75g caster sugar
2 cinnamon sticks
1 tsp cloves
3 star anise
1 tsp black peppercorns, lightly
  crushed
25g slightly salted butter
splash of Calvados
100ml apple juice
crème fraîche, to serve (optional)

Core the apples and pears using an apple corer, then peel off the skins. Cut the apples into quarters and halve the pears.

Scatter the sugar over the base of a wide, heavy-based non-stick frying pan and place over a high heat until it melts and begins to caramelise at the edges. Add the spices, followed by the butter. Tip the pan from side to side to mix the caramel and butter together. Take care as the mixture may spit and sputter.

Add the apples and pears to the pan cut side down. Cook for about 5–7 minutes until evenly caramelised, turning them several times. Carefully add a splash of Calvados, standing well back as the alcohol may flambé.

Pour in the apple juice and let bubble until the liquid has reduced and thickened to a syrupy sauce. Take off the heat and leave to cool slightly.

Divide the fruit among warm plates and spoon over the caramel sauce. Serve with a dollop of crème fraîche, if you like.

Quick flavour hits

Beyond the pepper mill, these are great flavour enhancers for quick meals:

Grated garlic   Save time chopping – instead grate peeled garlic cloves with a microplane or a small grater directly into the pan or bowl.

Curry salt   Mix 1 tsp curry powder to 2 tsp sea salt and use to add an extra kick to fish, shellfish, chicken and pork. We often sprinkle a little curry salt on to fresh scallops in the restaurants.

Flavoured oils   Brush a little chilli, rosemary or basil flavoured oil on grilled vegetables or drizzle over pasta before serving to lift the flavour. Buy good quality flavoured oils or make your own.

Flavoured butter Beat freshly chopped herbs and/ or spices (crushed garlic, paprika and saffron are my favourites) into softened salted butter, then roll in cling film and chill or freeze. Cut slices as required and dot on piping hot meat, fish or vegetables to pep up the flavour.

Herbed breadcrumbs Don't bin dry white bread. Cut off the crusts and whiz in a food processor with lots of herbs and some freshly grated Parmesan. Keep in the fridge or freezer and use as a tasty, colourful coating for fish fillets, lamb chops or chicken breasts.

*f*ast 5 salads

Salad of griddled asparagus & spinach
Minted melon, feta & fennel salad
Beetroot, goat's cheese & apple salad
Italian leafy salad with walnut dressing
Tangerine, frisée & sweet potato salad

450g asparagus, trimmed
5 tbsp olive oil
sea salt and black pepper
100g Roquefort or other blue cheese
1 tbsp Dijon mustard
2 tbsp cider vinegar
3 tbsp walnut oil, plus extra to drizzle
200g baby spinach leaves
50g walnut halves, toasted

(lower part of the stems). Toss with 2 tbsp olive oil and seasoning. Heat a griddle pan until hot. Add the asparagus spears and cook for 8 minutes, turning occasionally, until tender. Set aside.

Crumble half the cheese into a large bowl and crush with a fork, mixing in 1–2 tbsp water and the mustard to loosen it. Stir in the cider vinegar, then whisk in the walnut oil and the rest of the olive oil. Season with salt and pepper to taste. Toss through the spinach leaves and add a handful of the toasted walnuts.

Pile the spinach on to four plates. Cut the griddled asparagus spears in two on the diagonal, if you like, and arrange on top of the spinach. Crumble over the remaining cheese and walnuts. Drizzle with a little more walnut oil to serve.

Minted melon, feta & fennel salad

Serves 4

2 large fennel bulbs, trimmed and tough
   outer leaves removed
1 charentais (or ½ canteloupe) melon
100g mixed salad leaves
200g feta cheese
handful of mint leaves, finely shredded

DRESSING:
3 tbsp white wine vinegar
juice of ½ lemon
100ml olive oil
sea salt and black pepper

Slice the fennel as thinly as possible, using a mandolin if possible. Immerse in a bowl of iced water and set aside.

For the dressing, whisk together the wine vinegar, lemon juice and olive oil, and season with salt and pepper to taste.

Halve the melon, deseed and peel, then slice into long wedges. Cut these across into thin slices.

Drain the fennel, pat dry with kitchen paper and place in a salad bowl with the melon and salad leaves. Crumble over the feta. Add the shredded mint to the dressing and pour over the salad. Toss well and serve.

Beetroot, goat's cheese & apple salad

Serves 4

2 x 250g packs cooked baby beetroot
   in natural juice
1 Braeburn apple
squeeze of lemon juice
100g goat's cheese, crumbled
50g toasted hazelnuts, coarsely chopped

VINAIGRETTE:
2 tbsp balsamic vinegar
3 tbsp hazelnut (or walnut) oil
3 tbsp extra virgin olive oil
sea salt and black pepper

Whisk together the ingredients for the vinaigrette, seasoning with salt and pepper to taste.

Cut the baby beetroot into halves or quarters (wearing a pair of rubber gloves to avoid staining your hands). Quarter, core and thinly slice the apple and toss with a little lemon juice to stop it discolouring.

Pile the beetroot and apple slices on to four plates and scatter over the goat's cheese and hazelnuts. Drizzle with the vinaigrette and serve immediately.

Italian leafy salad with walnut dressing

Serves 4

2 heads of chicory, trimmed
1 small head of radicchio, trimmed
100g wild rocket

DRESSING:
50g walnuts halves, toasted
1 large garlic clove, peeled and grated
grated zest and juice of 1 lemon
6–8 tbsp extra virgin olive oil
sea salt and black pepper
2–3 tbsp freshly grated Parmesan

Finely slice the chicory and radicchio and put into a large salad bowl with the rocket leaves.

For the dressing, coarsely grind the walnuts together with the garlic and lemon zest, using a large pestle and mortar. Stir in the lemon juice, olive oil and seasoning to taste. Add the Parmesan and a little more olive oil or a splash of water, if you find the dressing is too thick.

Pour the dressing over the chicory, raddichio and rocket. Toss well and serve.

Tangerine, frisée & sweet potato salad

Serves 4

2 large sweet potatoes, peeled
sea salt and black pepper
2 tangerines
olive oil, to brush
1–2 tbsp orange or tangerine juice
50ml Classic Vinaigrette (see page 248)
200g frisée (curly endive)

Cut the sweet potatoes into 1cm thick rounds and boil in a pan of salted water for 3–4 minutes until they are just tender when pierced with a small sharp knife. Meanwhile, peel and segment the tangerines, removing the white pith.

Drain the potatoes well and pat dry with kitchen paper. Heat a griddle pan until hot. Griddle the sweet potato slices in several batches: brush with olive oil, sprinkle with salt and pepper, then griddle for 2–3 minutes on each side until charred.

For the dressing, whisk the orange or tangerine juice into the vinaigrette and check the seasoning.

Toss the frisée and tangerine segments with some of the dressing. Arrange on serving plates with the warm griddled potato slices. Trickle over the remaining dressing and serve.

Viva Italia!
{entertaining menu}

I love the Italian attitude to food – so long as you use the best and freshest ingredients, there is no need for complicated techniques or unnecessary frills. It is well exemplified in this menu. You might like to serve a leafy salad along with the main course, or to follow – as Italians would do. Serves 4.

planning your menu

Grilled sardines with gremolata
Veal piccata
Italian leafy salad (see page 66)
Easy tiramisu

- Prepare the tiramisu and chill.
- Make the gremolata, prepare the sardines and preheat the grill.
- Assemble the ingredients for the veal piccata.
- Grill and serve the sardines.
- Cook the veal, make the creamy sauce and serve.
- Follow with the salad (or serve alongside the main course).
- Top the tiramisu with a few sponge fingers and serve.

GRILLED SARDINES WITH GREMOLATA

"Zesty gremolata is the perfect foil for rich sardines. Like other oily fish, sardines spoil quickly so make sure they are very fresh when you buy them. Look for bright, clear eyes and firm flesh, and check that they smell faintly of the sea – definitely not of ammonia or too 'fishy'."

Serves 4
8 very fresh sardines, gutted and cleaned
olive oil, to drizzle
handful of rosemary sprigs, leaves only
1 lemon, halved

GREMOLATA:
100ml olive oil
2 garlic cloves, peeled and finely grated
grated zest and juice of 1 lemon
handful of flat leaf parsley, chopped
sea salt and black pepper

To make the gremolata, mix the olive oil, garlic, lemon zest and juice, and chopped parsley together in a bowl. Season with salt and pepper to taste. Set aside.

Pat the sardines dry with kitchen paper and rub all over with a little olive oil. Lay them side by side in a robust baking tray (or the grill pan) and season with salt and pepper. Preheat the grill to high.

Scatter the rosemary over the sardines and squeeze over some lemon juice. Grill for 4–5 minutes each side, basting the sardines with the pan juices as you turn them.

Transfer the sardines to a warm platter, spoon over the gremolata and serve immediately.

VEAL PICCATA

"Young tender veal chops are fantastic served with a tangy, creamy sauce. Traditionally, the sauce for veal piccata consists simply of white wine and capers, but I find crème fraîche adds a lovely, velvety richness to the sauce."

Serves 4
3 tbsp olive oil
1 head of garlic (unpeeled), halved crossways
4 British veal chops, about 270–300g each and 2.5–3cm thick
sea salt and black pepper
1 rosemary sprig
handful of thyme sprigs
200ml dry white wine
2 tbsp capers, drained
100ml crème fraîche

Heat the olive oil
in a wide, heavy-based pan and add the garlic halves, cut side down. Allow the garlic to infuse the oil over a medium-low heat for a minute, then increase the heat.

Season the veal chops
with salt and pepper and add to the pan. Throw in the herbs and fry the veal for 1½–2 minutes on each side until golden brown. Remove the veal from the pan and leave to rest on a warm plate for 5 minutes.

Pour off the excess oil
from the pan, then add the wine, scraping the bottom to deglaze. Bring to the boil and let bubble until reduced by half, adding any juices from the meat.

Stir in the capers
and crème fraîche and simmer for a minute or two until the sauce is the desired consistency. Season generously with salt and pepper to taste. Remove and discard the garlic and herbs.

Spoon the sauce
on to four warm plates and place the veal chops on top. Serve immediately, with some country bread on the side for mopping up the delicious sauce.

EASY TIRAMISU

" A good tiramisu makes a heavenly dessert but it is undoubtedly very rich and indulgent. For this quick, lighter version, single cream replaces eggs, though you can use double cream for a richer texture. **"**

Serves 4
150ml single cream
4 tbsp icing sugar
250g mascarpone
1 tsp vanilla extract
3 tbsp Marsala (or brandy or Tia Maria)
200ml strong coffee or espresso, cooled to room temperature
20–24 sponge fingers (savoiardi)
cocoa powder, to dust

Whip the cream with 3 tbsp icing sugar until evenly blended, then beat in the mascarpone, vanilla extract and 1 tbsp Marsala.

Sweeten the coffee with the remaining 1 tbsp icing sugar, stir to dissolve, then add the rest of the Marsala.

Dip 4 sponge fingers in the coffee mixture and use them to line the base of four serving glasses (breaking them into shorter lengths if necessary to fit the glasses). Spoon or pipe over a layer of the mascarpone mixture. Repeat layering the dipped sponge fingers and mascarpone mix until you reach the top of the glasses.

Spoon any remaining coffee mixture over the top and dust with sifted cocoa powder. Chill for at least 20 minutes.

Just before serving, stick two sponge fingers into each tiramisu.

fast 5 sandwiches

Crayfish, avocado & mayo toasties
Pata negra, melon & mozzarella focaccia
Roasted vegetable panini
Fresh tuna open sandwich
Smoked salmon & cream cheese on rye

Crayfish, avocado & mayo toasties

Serves 4

Toss 400g cooked crayfish tails with 4–5 tbsp mayonnaise and ½ tsp white truffle-infused olive oil. Stir through 1 chopped avocado and season with sea salt and black pepper to taste.

Lightly toast 4 thick slices of rustic white bread. Sandwich the crayfish filling between the toast slices and serve.

Pata negra, melon & mozzarella focaccia
Serves 4

Split 4 large pieces of focaccia (about 8 x 10cm) in half. Place the bottom halves on plates and top with a few thin slices of ripe cantaloupe or charentais melon.

Drape over a few slices of fresh buffalo mozzarella, 4 or 5 slices of pata negra ham and a few basil leaves.

Drizzle lightly with extra virgin olive oil, sprinkle with a little sea salt and grind over some black pepper. Sandwich together with the top focaccia halves and serve.

Roasted vegetable panini
Serves 4

Heat 2–3 tbsp olive oil in a wide frying pan. Fry 1 chopped red onion with a few thyme sprigs over a high heat for 3–4 minutes until it begins to soften. Tip in 1 chopped courgette and 1 each chopped red and yellow pepper. Cook for a few minutes, stirring often, until the vegetables are just tender. Season to taste.

Split 4 panini buns in half and spread both halves with pesto. Divide the vegetables among the bases and scatter over some shaved pecorino and a small handful of toasted pine nuts. Sandwich together with the panini tops.

Grill each sandwich in a panini press or toasted sandwich maker for a few minutes until compressed and warmed through.

TIP If you don't have a panini pan or toasted sandwich maker, wrap the paninis tightly in cling film, weigh down with a heavy tray for a while, then unwrap and griddle on both sides until warmed through.

Fresh tuna open sandwich

Serves 4

Season 2 thick tuna steaks and quickly sear in a very hot pan with a little olive oil, allowing 1½–2 minutes each side. Cool slightly. Trim 1 or 2 baby cos lettuce and separate the leaves. Toss in a bowl with a drizzle of olive oil and balsamic vinegar.

Toast 4 thick slices of crusty white bread and spread each with 1 tbsp tapenade or pesto. Lay on plates and pile the lettuce leaves on top. Thickly slice the tuna steaks and arrange over the lettuce. Sprinkle with a little sea salt, black pepper and olive oil, then serve.

Smoked salmon & cream cheese on rye

Serves 4

Season 200g cream cheese with ½ tsp cracked black pepper and a pinch of sea salt. Spread thickly on to 8 slices of rye bread. (Keep any remaining peppered cream cheese in the fridge for another sandwich.)

Lay 2 or 3 slices of smoked salmon on half of the bread slices, then top with a generous spoonful of oscietra caviar for a touch of luxury, if you like. Sandwich together with the rest of the bread slices and serve.

"Seasoning is especially important for fast dishes, which don't have long to develop a depth of flavour. I season a dish several times during cooking and always taste to check it at the end."

Fast fish & chips
{everyday menu}

After Sunday roast and curry, fish and chips must be the nation's favourite dish. Cod, haddock and plaice are traditional, or you can buy cheaper, more sustainable fish – like hake, whiting or coley. Coat in breadcrumbs and pan-fry, rather than deep-fry, for a healthy option and less clearing-up. Serves 4.

planning your menu

Pan-fried crumbed fish
+ Chunky chips   + Mushy peas
Strawberry shortbreads

- Preheat the oven.
- Cut the potatoes into chips and parboil them.
- Prepare the cream mix for the strawberry shortbreads and chill.
- Make the mushy peas and leave in the pan for reheating.
- Drain the potatoes, toss with the oil and flavourings and put into the oven.
- Coat the fish fillets, then fry until crisp.
- Serve the fish with the chips and mushy peas.
- Assemble the shortbreads to serve.

PAN-FRIED CRUMBED FISH

66 What you eat with fish and chips is a matter of personal taste. For me, it has to be a little malt vinegar and a generous sprinkling of salt, not forgetting a large mound of mushy peas on the side. 99

Serves 4
4 skinned white fish loin fillets
   (eg haddock, cod or coley), about
   170g each
75g plain flour
sea salt and black pepper
1 large egg, beaten
75g fresh breadcrumbs or Japanese
   panko breacrumbs (see tip)
3–4 tbsp olive oil
lemon wedges, to serve

TIP Japanese panko breadcrumbs are ideal to keep in the storecupboard to use as a fast substitute for fresh breadcrumbs.

Check the fish fillets for any pin bones, removing any you find with a pair of tweezers.

Tip the flour on to a plate and season with salt and pepper, mixing well. Pour the beaten egg into a shallow dish. Scatter the breadcrumbs on another plate.

Heat the olive oil in a large frying pan. Dip the fish fillets into the seasoned flour to coat, shaking off excess. Dip into the beaten egg, and finally into the breadcrumbs to coat evenly all over. Place in the hot frying pan and fry for about 5 minutes until golden and crisp all over, turning once.

Drain the fish on kitchen paper and serve immediately, with the chunky chips, mushy peas and lemon wedges for squeezing.

Chunky chips

Heat the oven to 220°C/Gas 7 and place a sturdy
roasting tray inside to heat up.

Cut the potatoes into 1cm thick chips. Par-boil
in a pan of salted water for about 5–7 minutes until just tender when
pierced with a skewer. Drain well and pat dry with a clean tea towel.

Tip the potatoes on to the hot roasting tray and
scatter over the garlic and herbs. Drizzle generously with olive oil and
sprinkle with salt and pepper. Toss the potatoes to coat in the oil and
flavourings, using a pair of tongs.

Bake in the oven for 10–15 minutes until the
chips are golden brown and crisp, turning them a few times. Drain on
kitchen paper and serve immediately.

Serves 4
1kg potatoes (eg Desirée or King Edward),
   scrubbed or peeled
sea salt and black pepper
5 garlic cloves (unpeeled)
few thyme sprigs
few rosemary sprigs (leaves only)
olive oil, to drizzle

Mushy peas

Serves 4
2 x 300g cans marrowfat peas
few knobs of butter
splash of white wine vinegar
sea salt and black pepper

Drain the peas, tip into a saucepan and lightly
crush with a fork or potato masher.

Place over a medium heat and stir
in the butter and a little splash of wine vinegar. Stir frequently for a few
minutes until the peas are heated through. Season with salt and
pepper to taste.

STRAWBERRY SHORTBREADS

"" These can be ready in a matter of minutes and they look impressive – even thrown together in a higgledy-piggledy manner for a casual supper. Just make sure you buy fine quality, thin shortbreads and assemble just before serving. ""

Serves 4

200ml crème fraîche

75ml double cream

2–3 tbsp icing sugar, plus extra to dust

8 all-butter round shortbreads

400g strawberries, hulled and quartered

few mint sprigs (leaves only), roughly shredded, plus a few sprigs to finish

Put the crème fraîche, double cream and 2 tbsp icing sugar into a large bowl. Beat lightly until smooth and just thick, taking care not to over-whisk. Taste and add a little more icing sugar, if you like.

Place a shortbread on each serving plate. Spoon a large dollop of the creamy mixture on top. Scatter the strawberries and mint over the cream.

Dust the remaining shortbreads with icing sugar and rest them on top of the strawberries. Add a mint sprig to each dessert and serve.

f ast
eggs

Bacon, pea & goat's cheese omelette
Poached duck egg with anchovy fingers
Scrambled eggs with crabmeat & chives
Baked egg florentine
Warm black pudding & quail's egg salad

Bacon, pea & goat's cheese omelette

Serves 4

20g butter

8 rashers of smoked streaky bacon, chopped

200g peas (thawed, if frozen)

few basil leaves, roughly sliced or torn

8 large eggs, beaten

150g goat's cheese log with rind, thickly sliced

sea salt and black pepper

Parmesan, for grating

large handful of rocket leaves

2–3 tbsp Classic Vinaigrette (see page 248)

Preheat the grill to its highest setting. Melt the butter in a large non-stick frying pan and fry the bacon until golden brown and crisp. Toss in the peas and cook for another minute or two, then add the basil.

Pour in the beaten eggs and gently shake the pan over medium heat. As the omelette begins to set at the bottom, top with the goat's cheese. Season generously with pepper and a little salt.

Grate some Parmesan over the omelette and place the pan under the hot grill for a minute or two until the eggs are set on top. Slide on to a warm large plate.

Toss a handful of rocket leaves in vinaigrette to dress lightly, then pile on top of the omelette. Cut into wedges to serve.

Poached duck egg with anchovy fingers

Serves 4

4 very fresh duck eggs, at room temperature
1 tsp white wine vinegar

ANCHOVY FINGERS:
2 tbsp tapenade
4 slices of medium sliced white bread
about 16 salted anchovies in oil, drained
3–4 tbsp olive oil

To be ready to poach the eggs, bring a wide, deep saucepan of water to a simmer and add the vinegar.

For the anchovy fingers, spread the tapenade on 2 slices of white bread and arrange the anchovies on top. Cover with the remaining bread slices, then flatten the sandwiches with a rolling pin and cut off the crusts. Heat the olive oil in a frying pan and fry the anchovy sandwiches until golden brown on both sides. Remove and drain on kitchen paper, then slice into 1cm wide fingers; keep warm.

Crack the duck eggs, one at a time, into a teacup and slide them into the slowly simmering water. Poach for 2–3 minutes until the whites are set and the yolks are still runny in the middle. With a slotted spoon, carefully remove each one and place in a small warm bowl. Serve with the anchovy fingers, for dipping into the runny yolk.

Scrambled eggs with crabmeat & chives

Serves 4

30g butter

12 large eggs, lightly beaten

200g white (or mixture of white and
   brown) crabmeat, picked through

handful of chives, finely chopped

sea salt and black pepper

2 tbsp crème fraîche

4 thick slices of country bread, toasted

Melt the butter in a non-stick saucepan and add the beaten eggs. Stir with a wooden spoon over a low heat for a few minutes until the eggs are half-set but still quite runny.

Stir in the crabmeat, chives and seasoning. Keep stirring until the eggs are just about to set, then quickly incorporate the crème fraîche and remove the pan from the heat.

Place a slice of toast on each warm plate and spoon the scrambled eggs on top. Serve immediately.

Baked egg florentine

30g butter
450g spinach leaves, washed and dried
sea salt and black pepper
4 large eggs, at room temperature
6–8 tbsp crème fraîche
nutmeg, for grating

Heat the oven to 200°C/Gas 6. Melt the butter in a large pan over a high heat. Add the spinach leaves and some seasoning and stir for a few seconds until the spinach has just wilted.

Divide the spinach among 4 buttered individual ceramic baking dishes and spread evenly, making a slight indentation in the centre. Leave to cool slightly.

Crack an egg into each indentation, then carefully spoon the crème fraîche around. Season with a sprinkling of salt, pepper and freshly grated nutmeg.

Bake in the oven for 10–12 minutes until the egg whites are set, but the yolks are still quite soft and runny in the centre. Serve immediately.

Warm black pudding & quail's egg salad

Serves 4

24 quail's eggs, at room temperature
200g black pudding
2–3 tbsp olive oil
75ml Classic Vinaigrette (see page 248)
200g mixed salad leaves
sea salt and black pepper

Bring a small pan of water to a gentle boil. Lower the quail's eggs into the water and cook for 2 minutes, then drain and refresh in a bowl of cold water. Peel off the shells and halve the eggs lengthways, if you like.

Thickly slice the black pudding into rounds. Heat the olive oil in a non-stick frying pan and fry the pudding slices for 2–3 minutes on each side. Add the quail's eggs to the pan to warm through briefly. Pour in the vinaigrette and quickly remove the pan from the heat.

Tip the pan contents into a large bowl containing the salad leaves. Toss lightly and season with a little salt and pepper. Pile on to individual plates to serve.

Outdoor eating
{entertaining menu}

There is nothing like sharing an al fresco meal with family and friends, either on a picnic blanket in a grassy meadow or just out in the back garden. The dishes on this menu are ideal for summer eating. The choice is yours whether you take them on a picnic or simply into the garden. Serves 4.

planning your menu

Tomato & pesto tart

Peppered lamb steaks
+ Green bean, red onion & pecorino salad

Macerated summer berries with clotted cream

Fresh lemonade

- Preheat the oven. Make the tart and put in the oven to bake.
- Blanch the green beans and salt the onion for the salad.
- Macerate the summer berries.
- Make the lemonade.
- Finish the salad.
- Fry the lamb steaks (and cool if taking on a picnic).
- Pack everything in containers to take on a picnic or arrange on platters to eat in the garden, leaving the dessert in the fridge until ready to serve.

TOMATO & PESTO TART

"To me, this tart – with its filling of vine-ripened tomatoes set against a background of fresh basil pesto – epitomises summer. For a different dimension, use walnuts in the pesto instead of pine nuts. The tart travels well if you're planning a picnic and it's delicious warm or cold."

Serves 4

250g puff pastry

plain flour, to dust

1 egg yolk, beaten with 1 tbsp water, to glaze

2–3 tbsp pesto (see page 249)

100g cherry tomatoes, halved

1 small rosemary sprig (leaves only), finely chopped

few thyme sprigs (leaves only)

2 spring onions, trimmed and finely sliced

2 tbsp freshly grated Parmesan

3–4 basil leaves, roughly chopped

olive oil, to drizzle

Heat the oven to 220°C/Gas 7. Roll out the puff pastry on a lightly floured surface to a large rectangle, about 15 x 25cm. Using a sharp knife, score a 1cm border around the edge, making sure you don't cut right through the pastry. Brush the border with egg glaze.

Spread 2–3 tbsp pesto over the pastry (within the border) and arrange the tomato halves on top. Scatter over the chopped rosemary and thyme, spring onions and grated Parmesan.

Bake for 20 minutes until the pastry is golden brown and crisp. Scatter over the chopped basil and drizzle with a little olive oil. Serve the tart warm or cold, cut into quarters.

PEPPERED LAMB STEAKS

" If you are eating in the garden, I suggest you serve the lamb still warm. Otherwise, for a picnic, take the cooked steaks with you; slice them thickly and scatter on top of the salad before applying the dressing. "

Serves 4
2–2½ tbsp black peppercorns
4 lamb leg steaks, each 250g and about 2cm thick
2 tbsp olive oil

Crush the peppercorns lightly,
using a pestle and mortar, then tip into a sieve and shake to get rid off the fine dust. Tip the crushed peppercorns on to a plate and press both sides of the steaks on to the peppercorns to coat.

Heat the olive oil in a large frying pan. Add the
lamb steaks and fry over a high heat for 2–3 minutes on each side. Remove from the pan and leave to rest for 5 minutes.

Slice the peppered lamb thickly and serve
alongside (or on top of) the salad. Serve warm or cold, with crusty bread.

Green bean, red onion & pecorino salad

Add the beans to a pan of boiling salted water and
cook for 4 minutes or until just tender. Drain, refresh in cold water, then pat dry with kitchen paper.

Put the onion in a colander, sprinkle with salt and
leave for 5 minutes. Holding the colander over the sink, pour on a kettleful of boiling water to remove some of the onion's acidity. Drain well and pat dry.

Toss the beans, onion and pecorino together in a
bowl. For the dressing, whisk together the olive oil, lemon juice and salt and pepper to taste (or shake to emulsify in a screw-topped jar).

Drizzle the dressing over the salad to serve.

Serves 4
400g green beans, trimmed
sea salt and black pepper
1 red onion, peeled and thinly sliced
50g pecorino, freshly grated
2–3 tbsp extra virgin olive oil
juice of ½ lemon

MACERATED SUMMER BERRIES
WITH CLOTTED CREAM

" This is my idea of summer in a bowl. Clotted cream is the ultimate indulgence, but you might prefer a scoop of vanilla ice cream or a dollop of crème fraîche. "

Serves 4

200g strawberries, hulled and
    quartered if large
450g other mixed berries
    (eg raspberries, redcurrants and
    blackberries)
2 tbsp icing sugar
150ml Muscat (or other sweet dessert
    wine)
clotted cream, to serve

Toss all of the berries together in a bowl with the icing sugar and Muscat. Cover and leave to macerate in the fridge for 15–20 minutes.

Divide the berries among individual bowls, spoon over the liquor and serve with a dollop of clotted cream.

Fresh lemonade

Squeeze the juice from the lemons and limes and strain into a large jug. Tip in the sugar and stir well to dissolve. Put the spent citrus skins into the jug with the basil and fill with ice cubes. Top up with cold water to taste.

Serves 4

2 lemons, halved
2 limes, halved
100g caster sugar
few basil sprigs
plenty of ice cubes

"Don't skip meals or resort to junk food, however busy you are. Keep some great stand-by ingredients in the fridge and freezer and you'll always be able to run up a speedy, nourishing working lunch."

fast working lunches

Pastrami & cream cheese bagel
Fusilli salad with merguez & olives
Leftover roast chicken salad
Rice noodle & smoked mackerel salad
Sausage & beans

Pastrami & cream cheese bagel

Serves 2

Split 2 poppyseed bagels in half. Lightly toast them if you're preparing lunch to eat straight away.

Mix 100g cream cheese with 1 tbsp wholegrain mustard and salt and pepper to taste. Spread evenly over the cut surfaces of the bagel halves.

Arrange 2 or 3 pastrami slices, a sliced large gherkin and a small handful of rocket leaves on each bagel base. Sandwich together with the bagel tops.

Fusilli salad with merguez & olives
Serves 2

Cook 150g fusilli in a pan of well salted water for 10–12 minutes or until al dente.

In the meantime, thinly slice 200g merguez sausages on the diagonal. Heat 2 tbsp olive oil in a frying pan and fry the sausage slices over a medium heat until golden brown. Toss through 50g sun-dried tomatoes and 100g quartered pitted olives. Warm through for a minute or two, then take off the heat.

Drain the pasta and toss with the sausage mix. Taste and adjust the seasoning. Stir through a handful of chopped mixed herbs, such as flat leaf parsley, chives and basil. Serve warm or cold.

Leftover roast chicken salad
Serves 2

Trim 200g watercress, removing the stalks, then wash and dry well on kitchen paper. Slice or shred the meat from ½ roast chicken (perhaps leftover from yesterday's roast).

For the dressing, mix the juice of ½ lemon with 6 tbsp extra virgin olive oil, adding any pan juices from the roast chicken and salt and pepper to taste. Toss the chicken in the dressing.

Add the watercress to the chicken just before serving and toss to mix. Serve with lemon wedges on the side and a few chunks of crusty baguette.

TIP If you're taking the salad to work, pack the watercress and chicken in separate containers and toss together at lunchtime.

Rice noodle & smoked mackerel salad
Serves 2

Put a 65g bundle of rice noodles into a large bowl, pour over boiling water to cover and leave to soak for 10 minutes. Blanch 100g trimmed sugar snap peas in a pan of salted water for 2 minutes until still slightly crunchy. Drain and refresh under cold running water, then slice in half, if you like.

Mix 1 tbsp grated fresh ginger with the juice of ½ lime and 1 tbsp each light soy sauce, fish sauce, mirin and sesame oil. Drain the noodles well, then toss with the sugar snaps and dressing.

Flake 100g hot-smoked mackerel (coated in peppercorns) into large pieces and scatter over the dressed rice noodles and sugar snaps. Sprinkle with 2 tbsp toasted sesame seeds and a finely sliced spring onion. Serve cold.

Sausage & beans

Fry 4 Toulouse sausages in a wide, heavy-based pan with 2 tbsp olive oil and a few thyme sprigs. Add 2 finely sliced garlic cloves and cook for 3–4 minutes, stirring occasionally, until the sausages are golden brown.

Tip in a 400g can mixed beans (drained and rinsed), then a 400g can chopped tomatoes. Bring to a simmer, partially cover and stew for 10–12 minutes, by which time the sausages should be cooked through.

TIP Prepare ahead, cool and pack in a rigid plastic container. Reheat in the microwave at work or in a pan over a low heat.

Season with salt, pepper and a pinch of sugar if the tomato sauce is too sharp. Serve in bowls with chunks of crusty bread.

Mexican flavours

Fajitas are fantastic for a casual midweek meal that you can eat with your hands. Get everyone involved in making them: someone to slice the peppers and beef; another to make the guacamole; and a third to prepare the dessert. Supper will be ready in no time. Serves 4.

planning your menu

Beef fajitas with soured cream & guacamole
Melon with tequila & lime

- Prepare the melon and steep in the tequila lime dressing in the fridge.
- Put four serving glasses in the fridge to chill.
- Slice the beef and peppers and toss them with the spice mix.
- Make the guacamole and set aside.
- Fry the beef and peppers and warm up the tortillas.
- Assemble the fajitas and serve.
- Divide the melon among glasses, top with lime zest and mint, then serve.

BEEF FAJITAS
WITH SOURED CREAM & GUACAMOLE

The spice mix I use here for the beef and peppers is quite fiery, but you can easily tone it down if you're catering for young children who can't take the heat. Simply replace the chilli powder with ground coriander.

Serves 4

600g beef fillet
1 red pepper
2 yellow peppers
1 tsp ground cumin
½ tsp hot (or medium) chilli powder
½ tsp paprika
sea salt and black pepper
3 tbsp olive oil
6–8 plain tortillas
6–8 tbsp soured cream
few coriander sprigs (leaves only),
   roughly torn

GUACAMOLE:
2 medium ripe avocados
juice of 1 lime
1 garlic clove, peeled and finely grated
½ red chilli, deseeded and finely chopped
1 shallot, peeled and finely chopped
2 ripe plum tomatoes, finely chopped
handful of coriander (leaves only),
   chopped

TIP Make up a quantity of spice mix and keep in a sealed jar, ready to use for fajitas or a spicy stir-fry whenever you fancy.

Slice the beef into long, thin strips and place in a bowl. Halve, core and deseed the peppers, then cut into strips.

In a small jar, mix together the cumin, chilli powder, paprika, salt and pepper. Add half the spice mix to the beef strips and mix well. Add the rest to the sliced peppers and toss to coat. Set aside to marinate.

To make the guacamole, halve the avocados and remove the stones. Scoop the flesh into a bowl, add the lime juice and lightly mash with a fork until you get a chunky paste. Add the garlic, chilli, shallot, tomatoes and coriander. Mix well and season with salt and pepper to taste. Set aside.

Heat a large wok and add the olive oil. When it is very hot, tip in the peppers and sauté until they are slightly soft, then toss in the beef strips. Cook for 2 minutes, stirring and tossing frequently, until the beef is just cooked. Remove from the wok and keep warm.

Warm up the tortillas in a dry frying pan for about 10 seconds each side. Put some beef and peppers along the centre of each tortilla and add a dollop of soured cream and some guacamole. Scatter over some torn coriander and roll up. Serve immediately.

MELON WITH TEQUILA & LIME

"Fragrant honeydew melon tossed in a tequila, honey and lime dressing is the perfect refreshing dessert after a meal of spicy fajitas. If you don't possess a melon baller, simply cut the melon into thin slices and drizzle with the dressing."

Serves 4

1 honeydew melon, preferably chilled
2–3 tbsp cold tequila
finely grated zest of ½ lime, plus extra to serve
juice of ½ lime
2–3 tbsp runny honey
tiny pinch of fine sea salt
few mint sprigs (leaves only), chopped

Halve the melon and remove the seeds with a spoon. Using a melon baller, scoop the flesh into neat balls and place in a large bowl.

Mix the tequila, lime zest and juice, honey and salt together in a small jug. Taste and add a little more honey if the dressing is too sour. Pour over the melon balls, toss gently to mix and chill for at least 10–15 minutes.

Divide the melon balls among serving glasses, grate over some lime zest and sprinkle with freshly chopped mint to serve.

fast pasta 5

Spaghetti with anchovy, garlic & parsley
Pappardelle, smoked trout & tomatoes
Linguine with tomatoes, olives & capers
Penne, runner beans & goat's cheese
Pasta with pancetta, leek & mushrooms

Spaghetti with anchovy, garlic & parsley

Serves 4

300g dried spaghetti
sea salt and black pepper
3 tbsp olive oil, plus extra to drizzle
2 garlic cloves, peeled and thinly sliced
200g pack freshly marinated anchovies,
　roughly chopped
bunch of flat leaf parsley, roughly
　chopped
freshly grated Parmesan, to serve

Cook the spaghetti in boiling salted water for 8–10 minutes or until al dente.

Heat the olive oil in a large pan, in the meantime. Add the garlic and fry over a medium heat until golden brown at the edges. Stir in the chopped anchovies.

Drain the spaghetti and tip into the pan with the garlic and anchovies. Add the chopped parsley and season to taste with salt and pepper. Toss well.

Divide among warm bowls and serve with grated Parmesan and a drizzle of olive oil.

Pappardelle, smoked trout & tomatoes

Serves 4

6 vine-ripened plum tomatoes

sea salt and black pepper

15 semi-dried tomatoes in oil (about 85g)

2 garlic cloves, peeled and roughly chopped

2 banana shallots (or 4 regular ones), peeled and roughly chopped

175ml olive oil

juice of ½ lemon

500g fresh pappardelle or tagliatelle

600g skinless smoked trout fillets, flaked into large chunks

Parmesan, for grating

Add the plum tomatoes to a large pan of boiling salted water and blanch for 2 minutes. Lift out with a slotted spoon to a bowl of iced water to cool for a few minutes, then remove and peel off the skins. Halve the tomatoes and squeeze out the seeds.

Put the tomatoes into a food processor along with the semi-dried tomatoes, garlic, shallots, olive oil and lemon juice. Whiz to a smooth sauce and season to taste. Pour the sauce into a pan and warm through over a medium-high heat while you cook the pasta.

Cook the pasta in boiling salted water (the pan you used for the tomatoes) for 2 minutes until al dente. Drain well, then toss with the tomato dressing and flaked trout. Divide among warm plates and grate over some Parmesan to serve.

Linguine with tomatoes, olives & capers

Serves 4

300g dried linguine or spaghetti

sea salt and black pepper

3 tbsp olive oil, plus extra to drizzle

2 large garlic cloves, peeled and finely chopped

1 large red onion, peeled and chopped

1 red chilli, deseeded and finely sliced

6–8 anchovies in oil, drained and finely chopped

200g pitted black olives, quartered or chopped

3 tbsp capers, rinsed and drained

250g cherry tomatoes, halved

handful of basil leaves, shredded

Add the pasta to a pot of boiling salted water and cook for 8–10 minutes or until al dente.

Meanwhile, heat the olive oil in a wide pan and fry the garlic, onion, chilli and anchovies for 1–2 minutes. Add the olives, capers and tomatoes, and stir over a high heat for a few more minutes until the onions are soft.

Drain the pasta and toss with the sauce and shredded basil. Taste and adjust the seasoning (salt probably won't be needed because the anchovies, capers and olives are quite salty).

Divide among warm bowls and drizzle over a little more olive oil, if you wish, before serving.

Penne, runner beans & goat's cheese

Serves 4

300g dried penne (or other pasta shapes)
sea salt and black pepper
75g butter
1 red chilli, trimmed, deseeded and finely chopped
few rosemary sprigs (leaves only), chopped
250g runner beans, trimmed and sliced on the diagonal
extra virgin olive oil, to drizzle
150g soft rindless goat's cheese log
50g toasted pine nuts

Add the pasta to a large pan of boiling salted water and cook until al dente, about 8–10 minutes.

Meanwhile, melt the butter in a large pan, add the chilli and rosemary and warm over a low heat for 1–2 minutes to let the flavours infuse. Turn up the heat, add the runner beans and cook for 3–4 minutes, stirring occasionally, until they are tender.

Drain the pasta and toss with a little olive oil, then mix with the beans. Off the heat, crumble in the cheese and toss to mix, adding a splash of boiling water if the sauce is too thick. Season with salt and pepper to taste, scatter over the pine nuts and serve.

Pasta with pancetta, leek & mushrooms

Serves 4

300g dried pasta shells (conchiglie)
sea salt and black pepper
3–4 tbsp olive oil
125g pancetta, sliced
2 medium leeks, trimmed and finely sliced
250g chestnut mushrooms, trimmed and sliced
2–3 tbsp crème fraîche
bunch of flat leaf parsley, chopped

Add the pasta shells to a pot of boiling salted water and cook for 8–10 minutes or until al dente.

Meanwhile, heat the olive oil in a large frying pan and add the pancetta. Fry for a few minutes until golden brown, then add the leeks, mushrooms and a little salt and pepper. Stir over a high heat for 6–8 minutes until the leeks are tender.

Drain the pasta and immediately toss with the leeks, pancetta and mushrooms, and the crème fraîche. Season with salt and pepper to taste. Scatter over the chopped parsley to serve.

"For me, cooking and eating seasonally is a joy. Home-grown foods at their peak of perfection are best prepared simply with the minimum of cooking."

Easy for a crowd
{everyday menu}

Cooking for a larger number needn't be time-consuming. The secret is to keep things simple. If you possibly can, prepare some of the food in advance – make the ragout and/or the cheesecake up to a day ahead, or at least chop up the vegetables well in advance. Serves 8.

Baked chicken with aubergine, courgette
    & tomato ragout
No-bake berry cheesecake

- Preheat the oven. Prepare and chop the vegetables for the ragout.
- Make the biscuit topping for the dessert and chill.
- Line 8 ramekins with cling film for the cheesecakes.
- Whip up the creamy cheese filling, fill the ramekins and chill.
- Season and sear the chicken breasts, then set aside.
- Cook the vegetables in the pan.
- Put the chicken and vegetables into the oven.
- Soften the blueberries and leave to cool.
- Rest the chicken, then serve the main course.
- Unmould the cheesecakes, add the topping and berries, then serve.

BAKED CHICKEN
WITH AUBERGINE, COURGETTE & TOMATO RAGOUT

"Chicken breasts are quickly seared, then baked on Mediterranean vegetables for a great one-pot dish. For convenience, you can make the ragout well in advance, but for best results, bake the chicken breasts just before serving."

Serves 8

5 tbsp olive oil, plus extra to oil

8 large skinless chicken breasts

sea salt and black pepper

4 banana shallots, peeled and roughly
   chopped

4 garlic cloves (unpeeled), smashed

2 medium aubergines, trimmed and
   chopped

handful of thyme sprigs

handful of rosemary sprigs

4 courgettes, trimmed and chopped

glass of dry white wine

8 plum tomatoes, peeled, deseeded and
   chopped, or 400g canned chopped
   tomatoes

Heat the oven to 190°C/Gas 5. Heat a large heavy-based frying pan and add 3 tbsp olive oil. Season the chicken breasts with salt and pepper.

Sear the chicken in batches: cook skinned side down for 3–4 minutes until golden brown, then turn over and cook the other side for 2–3 minutes. Transfer to a plate.

Add the remaining oil to the pan and tip in the shallots, garlic, aubergines and a few thyme and rosemary sprigs. Cook for 5–7 minutes, stirring occasionally, until the onions are soft and translucent, and the aubergines are starting to soften. Season generously with salt and pepper.

Add the courgettes, then pour in the wine and simmer until it has reduced by half. In the meantime, put an oiled large roasting pan in the oven to warm up.

Stir the tomatoes through the vegetables and tip into the roasting pan. Place the seared chicken breasts on top and scatter over some more herb sprigs. Bake in the oven for 5–10 minutes, depending on the thickness of the chicken, until firm and cooked through.

Rest for 5 minutes before serving on warm plates, with plenty of crusty bread on the side.

NO-BAKE
BERRY CHEESECAKE

66 To be contrary, I've inverted the classic components of a cheesecake, topping the vanilla cream cheese with a biscuit topping and serving glazed blueberries on the side. If you haven't time to shape individual cheesecakes in ramekins, just layer the vanilla cream cheese and blueberries in glasses and scatter the crumb mix on top. 99

Serves 8
TOPPING:
8 digestive biscuits
6 tbsp caster sugar
100g unsalted butter

BERRIES:
300g blueberries (or blackberries)
2 tbsp caster sugar
splash of crème de cassis or water

VANILLA CREAM CHEESE:
400g cream cheese
6 tbsp icing sugar
juice of ½ lemon
1 vanilla pod, split
600ml double cream

TO FINISH:
icing sugar, to dust

For the topping, coarsely grind the biscuits in a food processor. Melt the sugar in a heavy-based non-stick pan until it begins to caramelise, then carefully add the butter, shaking the pan to mix the caramel with the butter as it melts. Add the crushed biscuits and toss to coat in the caramel. Tip on to a plate, chill for 5 minutes until firm, then break into pieces. Wipe out the pan with kitchen paper.

Tip the blueberries into the pan and sprinkle with the 2 tbsp sugar and a splash of cassis or water. Cook over a medium-high heat for a minute until the blueberries are slightly soft. Spread out on a plate and leave to cool.

For the vanilla cream cheese, put the cream cheese, icing sugar and lemon juice in a large bowl. Add the seeds from the vanilla pod and beat until smooth. In another bowl, lightly whip the cream to soft peaks, then fold into the cream cheese mixture.

To shape individual cheesecakes, line 8 ramekins with cling film. Fill with the cream cheese mixture and level the tops with the back of a knife. Chill until ready to serve.

Turn out the cheesecakes on to serving plates and remove the cling film. Scatter the topping over and spoon the blueberries around the plate. Dust with icing sugar and serve immediately.

shellfish

Mussels in an aromatic coconut broth
Crab spring rolls
Oyster shooters
Easy lobster thermidor
Prawns with orange & tequila

Mussels in an aromatic coconut broth

Serves 4

3 tbsp olive oil
2kg fresh mussels, scrubbed clean
(beards removed)
2 garlic cloves (unpeeled), halved
few thyme sprigs
100ml dry white wine
400g can coconut milk
1 lemongrass stalk, halved lengthways
1 red chilli, thinly sliced on the diagonal
2 spring onions, trimmed and finely
sliced on the diagonal
sea salt and black pepper
coriander leaves, to finish

Heat a large heavy-based saucepan with a tight-fitting lid until it is very hot, then add the olive oil. Quickly tip in the mussels, garlic, thyme and wine. Cover the pan with the lid and let the mussels steam for 3–4 minutes until they are fully opened.

Drain the mussels over a bowl to catch the liquor, then pour it into a clean pan and boil to reduce by half. Add the coconut milk, lemongrass, chilli, spring onions and seasoning. Bring to a simmer and let bubble for 2 minutes.

Meanwhile, discard any unopened mussels and the garlic, then divide the mussels among warm serving bowls. Ladle the hot coconut broth over the mussels, picking out and discarding the lemongrass. Scatter over some coriander leaves to serve.

Crab spring rolls

Serves 4

8 large spring roll wrappers (about
   25cm square)
1 large egg white, for brushing
groundnut oil, for deep-frying
sweet chilli sauce (see page 249),
   for dipping

FILLING:
250g white crabmeat
2 spring onions, trimmed and finely
   sliced
small handful of coriander leaves,
   chopped
1 tbsp wholegrain mustard
1½ tbsp mayonnaise
sea salt and black pepper
tiny squeeze of lime juice

TIP Spring roll wrappers are
easy to use. Most Asian food stores and
some supermarkets now stock them.

For the filling, toss all the ingredients together in a bowl
until evenly combined, adding salt, pepper and lime juice to taste.

Lay a spring roll wrapper on a board with a
corner facing you. (Keep the rest covered with a tea towel to prevent
them drying out.) Spoon 2 tbsp of the crabmeat filling on to the bottom
of the wrapper (as shown), then brush the surrounding pastry with egg
white. Fold the bottom edge up over the filling, brush the sides with
more egg white and fold them in and over the filling, like an envelope.
Roll up into a log. Repeat with the rest of the wrappers and filling.

Heat the oil for deep-frying (at least a 6cm depth) in a
suitable pan to 180°C. To check the oil is hot enough, drop in a cube of
bread – it should sizzle vigorously. Deep-fry the rolls in batches for
40–50 seconds until golden brown and crisp. Drain on kitchen paper.

Cut the spring rolls in half on the diagonal and
serve warm, with a bowl of sweet chilli sauce on the side for dipping.

Oyster shooters
Serves 4

50ml tomato juice, chilled
squeeze of lemon juice
generous dash of Worcestershire sauce
generous dash of Tabasco sauce
2 shots (about 50ml) cold vodka
4 fresh oysters
sea salt and black pepper
celery salt, for dipping (optional)
squeeze of lime juice (optional)

In a small jug, mix together the tomato juice, lemon juice, Worcestershire sauce, Tabasco and vodka. Shuck the oysters and add the natural juices to the tomato mixture. Season with salt and pepper to taste. Tip some celery salt into a small bowl or plate, if using.

Wet the rims of four shot glasses with a little water or lime juice, then dip in the celery salt to coat, if you like. Carefully pour the tomato mixture into the glasses to three-quarters fill them. Drop an oyster into each glass and serve immediately.

TIP To shuck an oyster, hold in a folded tea towel and insert an oyster knife through the hinge of the shell. Keeping the oyster level, wriggle the knife to sever the hinge muscle, then push it in a bit further and twist up to lift the top shell. Tip the juice into a bowl and remove any pieces of shell from the oyster. Slide the knife along the bottom shell to release the oyster.

140

Easy lobster thermidor

Serves 4

2 freshly cooked lobsters
Parmesan, for grating
small handful of chives and chervil,
 chopped

SAUCE:
100g crème fraîche
2 egg yolks
1 tsp dry English mustard
sea salt and black pepper

Uncurl the lobster tails and place them flat on a board. Using a strong pair of kitchen scissors, snip along the bottom shells, then use a large knife to cut the tails into two halves. Remove the flesh and place back into the shells, the other way around.

To prepare the claws, pull out the small claw to release the blade, then crack open the shells of the thick claws with the back of a knife. Gently pull out the flesh and place on a baking tray, along with the lobster tails.

Heat the grill to its highest setting. Mix the ingredients for the sauce together, then spoon over the lobster tails and claws. Grate over a little Parmesan and grill for 3–4 minutes until golden brown on top. Serve immediately, with a sprinkling of chopped herbs.

Prawns with orange & tequila

Serves 4

3 tbsp olive oil
400g fresh tiger prawns
2 garlic cloves, peeled and finely sliced
sea salt and black pepper
generous splash of tequila
juice of 1 orange, or 2 clementines

Heat a large frying pan, then add the olive oil.
When hot, add the prawns with the garlic and some seasoning. Fry for 2 minutes on each side until the prawns turn bright red and opaque.

Add a splash of tequila, carefully and
standing well back as it may flambé. Pour in the orange juice and let bubble for a few minutes until the liquid has reduced. Transfer to a warm plate and serve immediately.

"However amazing a dish looks, it is always the taste that lingers in your memory. Family and friends will appreciate a meal that tastes superb – even if you've brought the pan to the table."

tapas spread
{entertaining menu}

Feasting on a selection of smaller dishes is popular in many parts of the world – Chinese dim sum, Middle Eastern mezze and Spanish tapas are all examples. This menu is based on some of my favourite tapas. They are all quick to make and you can add bowls of Spanish olives and salted Marcona almonds to extend the spread. Serves 4.

planning your menu

Fried chorizo with parsley
Sautéed prawns with green peppercorns
Manchego & membrillo on olive bread
Iberian ham with garlic & chickpeas
Squid with olives

- Assemble the manchego tapas. Arrange on a platter and keep covered.
- Fry the chorizo and toss with the parsley; keep warm.
- Fry the garlic and chickpeas; keep warm.
- Cook the squid and olives.
- Sauté the prawns with paprika and green peppercorns.
- Assemble the ham, garlic and chickpeas on a platter.
- Plate the other tapas in warm bowls to serve.

FRIED CHORIZO WITH PARSLEY

" If you can, buy fresh chorizo from a good butcher or deli for this dish. Serve the fried chorizo as it is, or pile on to crusty bread slices and drizzle with the orange-coloured oil from the pan. **"**

Serves 4
250g chorizo sausage
2 tbsp olive oil
squeeze of lemon juice
handful of flat leaf parsley (leaves only),
   roughly chopped

Peel away the skin from the chorizo, then chop the sausage into bite-sized chunks.

Heat the olive oil in a frying pan. Add the chorizo and fry, tossing frequently, over a high heat for 2 minutes or until it has released its oils and is browned at the edges.

Add the lemon juice and stir in the chopped parsley. Serve warm.

SAUTEED PRAWNS
WITH GREEN PEPPERCORNS

" Paprika and green peppercorns give prawns a vibrant piquancy. I like to use Madagascar green peppercorns (usually sold brined in small cans) for their slightly spicy, tangy flavour. Buy good quality cooked prawns in the shell from your fishmonger or supermarket fresh fish counter. **"**

Heat the olive oil in a large frying pan until hot. Pat the prawns dry, then tip into the pan. Sprinkle with the paprika, add a pinch of salt and fry for 1 minute, tossing occasionally.

Add the peppercorns and lemon juice to the pan and sauté for another 30 seconds. Transfer the prawns to a bowl and serve warm.

Serves 4
1 tbsp olive oil
200g cooked prawns in the shell
½ tsp paprika
sea salt
1–2 tbsp green peppercorns, drained
juice of ½ lemon

MANCHEGO & MEMBRILLO
ON OLIVE BREAD

“ I love the combination of salty cheese and sweet membrillo in this classic tapa. Membrillo, a Spanish-style quince jelly, is increasingly easy to find in good delis and supermarkets. You can buy it in blocks that you slice, or in softer pastes that can be spread on toasts. Similarly manchego cheese is relatively easy to obtain. ”

Serves 4
4 thin slices of olive bread
150g manchego cheese
8 tsp membrillo paste
extra virgin olive oil, to drizzle
sea salt and black pepper

TIP Try other toppings to add variety to your tapas spread, such as jamon and piquillo peppers, or marinated anchovies and sliced manzanilla olives.

Cut each slice of bread into four. Cut the manchego cheese into medium slices and remove any outer rind.

Place a slice of cheese on each bread slice and top with a spoonful of membrillo paste. (If using firm membrillo, cut into thin slices and place on top of the cheese.)

Drizzle with a little olive oil and sprinkle with sea salt and a grinding of black pepper. Arrange the tapas on a serving platter.

IBERIAN HAM WITH GARLIC & CHICKPEAS

"It is quite common to pair savoury Iberian ham with pulses in Spain. This recipe uses chickpeas but you could substitute canned cooked cannellini, flageolet or borlotti beans, whichever you have to hand."

Serves 4
2 tbsp olive oil
2 garlic cloves, peeled and thinly sliced
100g canned chickpeas, drained and
   rinsed
sea salt and black pepper
8 slices Iberian ham

Heat the olive oil in a frying pan over a low heat. Add the garlic slices and cook for a minute to allow the flavours to infuse. Tip in the chickpeas, increase the heat to medium and season with salt and pepper to taste. Warm through, stirring occasionally, then take the pan off the heat.

Drape the ham slices on a serving platter and spoon over the chickpeas, garlic and oil from the pan. Serve warm.

SQUID WITH OLIVES

"This is a wonderfully simple way to cook baby squid. The vinaigrette imparts a zesty flavour and helps to tenderise the squid."

Serves 4
250g baby squid (about 6–8), cleaned
50g black olives
50ml extra virgin olive oil
50ml groundnut oil
juice of ½ lemon
sea salt and black pepper
small handful of flat leaf parsley, roughly
   chopped

Rinse the squid and pat dry. Slice the body into thin rings and place these in a saucepan with the tentacles.

Add the olives, oils, lemon juice and seasoning. Slowly bring the liquid to the boil, then immediately turn off the heat. Cover and leave the squid to continue cooking in the residual heat of the vinaigrette. The squid is ready when it turns white and opaque.

Stir the chopped parsley through the squid then, with a slotted spoon, transfer to a serving bowl. Drizzle over a little of the warm vinaigrette to serve.

fast vegetarian

Gratin of roasted peppers, basil & feta

Serves 4

2 x 450g jars ready-roasted peppers
   (ideally mixed red and yellow peppers)
large bunch of basil
2 x 200g packs feta cheese
black pepper
olive oil, to drizzle
Parmesan, for grating

Heat the oven to 220°C/Gas 7. Drain the peppers and slice in half if they are whole.

Arrange a layer of peppers in four small individual gratin dishes. Top with a handful of basil leaves, then crumble over a layer of feta. Season with pepper and drizzle with olive oil. Repeat these layers to reach the top of the dishes.

Grate some Parmesan over the top and grind over a little more pepper. Bake for 8–10 minutes or until the cheese is golden brown on top.

Quick minestrone

3–4 tbsp olive oil
1 onion, peeled and diced
1 waxy potato, peeled and diced
1 medium carrot, peeled and diced
1 kohlrabi, peeled and diced
2 bay leaves
few thyme sprigs
75g dried spaghetti, broken into pieces
¼ Savoy cabbage, cored and chopped
sea salt and black pepper
handful of flat leaf parsley, chopped
75g Parmesan, freshly grated

Heat the olive oil in a large saucepan and add the onion, potato, carrot, kohlrabi and herbs. Cook, stirring frequently, over a high heat for 8–10 minutes until the vegetables are soft. Meanwhile, put the kettle on to boil.

Pour enough hot water over the vegetables to cover them and bring back to the boil. Add the spaghetti to the soup along with the cabbage and simmer for a further 8 minutes or until the spaghetti is al dente.

Season the soup liberally and sprinkle generously with chopped parsley and grated Parmesan just before serving.

Nutty bulgar wheat with herbs
Serves 4

300g bulgar wheat
75g shelled pistachio nuts, toasted
large handful of mixed herbs (eg flat leaf
    parsley, chervil, mint and basil)
1½ tbsp pomegranate molasses
1½ tbsp lemon juice
6 tbsp extra virgin olive oil, plus extra
    to drizzle (optional)
sea salt and black pepper

Put the bulgar wheat into a saucepan and pour over boiling water (from the kettle) to cover. Simmer for 10–12 minutes or until the grains are just tender. Meanwhile, coarsely chop the pistachio nuts and herbs.

For the dressing, mix the pomegranate molasses, lemon juice and olive oil together in a bowl. Season with salt and pepper to taste.

Drain the bulgar wheat thoroughly when it's ready, then immediately toss with the dressing, pistachios and herbs. Taste and adjust the seasoning, and drizzle with a little more oil, if you wish. Serve warm or as a cold salad.

Easy vegetable curry

2 tbsp vegetable oil

1 banana shallot (or 2 regular ones), peeled and roughly chopped

1 garlic clove, peeled and finely chopped

2 long red chillies, deseeded and finely chopped

1 small celeriac, peeled and chopped

sea salt and black pepper

3 tbsp Madras curry paste

few cardamom pods

1 green pepper, cored, deseeded and roughly chopped

½ large cauliflower, cut into florets

400g can chopped tomatoes

½ head of broccoli, cut into florets

1 large courgette, roughly chopped

about 250ml Greek-style natural yogurt

Heat the oil in a large, wide pan and add the shallot, garlic and chillies. Cook, stirring, for a minute or so until the garlic is fragrant.

Add the celeriac and some seasoning. Cook over a high heat for 2 minutes, then add the curry paste, cardamom pods, green pepper and cauliflower florets. Continue to stir over a high heat for a few more minutes.

Tip in the tomatoes, then fill the empty can with water and pour this in too. Bring to the boil, then add the broccoli and courgette. Simmer for 8–10 minutes until the vegetables are tender.

Turn down the heat and stir in the yogurt. Taste and adjust the seasoning before serving.

Ratatouille

Serves 4

1 large red onion, peeled
1 small aubergine
1 red pepper, halved, cored and deseeded
1 yellow pepper, halved, cored and deseeded
1 large courgette
4 tbsp olive oil
few thyme sprigs
sea salt and black pepper
1 fat garlic clove, peeled and smashed
400g can chopped tomatoes
225g vine-ripened cherry tomatoes
small handful of basil leaves, roughly torn

Chop the vegetables into bite-sized pieces, keeping them separate. Heat the olive oil in a large pan and sauté the onion with the thyme sprigs and a little seasoning over a high heat for a minute or two.

Add the aubergine, red and yellow peppers, and the garlic. Sauté for a minute, then add the courgette and fry for another 2 minutes or so.

Tip in the canned tomatoes and add a splash of water. Now add the cherry tomatoes and bring to a simmer. Cook for 8–10 minutes until the vegetables are just tender.

Season the ratatouille with salt and pepper to taste, and sprinkle with basil before serving.

Cheap & cheerful
{everyday menu}

This easy menu is designed with a young family in mind. I don't know any child (or adult) who doesn't like chicken and flavourful mash. But the trick is always with the pudding. Promise your kids a banana split they cannot resist if they eat up their main course – it works like a charm with my lot. Serves 4.

Sticky lemon chicken
+ Champ + green beans or sugar snap peas
Caramelised banana split

- Caramelise the bananas and make the chocolate sauce.
- Put the potatoes on to boil for the champ.
- Brown the chicken pieces, add the sauce ingredients and leave to reduce.
- Drain the potatoes, make the champ and keep warm.
- Serve the sticky lemon chicken and champ when ready.
- Assemble the caramelised banana splits just before serving.

STICKY LEMON CHICKEN

" If you have a jar of preserved lemons in the cupboard, chop up a lemon and add it to the sauce with a little more honey before reducing. It will give the dish a different dimension. "

Serves 4

1 large chicken, jointed into 8–10 pieces
sea salt and black pepper
3–4 tbsp olive oil
1 head of garlic, halved horizontally
few thyme sprigs
splash of sherry vinegar
2 tbsp dark soy sauce
3 tbsp honey
1 lemon, finely sliced (ideally with a
   mandolin)
bunch of flat leaf parsley, chopped

Season the chicken
with salt and pepper and heat the olive oil in a large sauté pan. Brown the chicken pieces (in batches if necessary) over a high heat with the garlic and thyme for 2–3 minutes on each side until golden brown. Return all the chicken to the pan, add the sherry vinegar and bubble until reduced by half. Drizzle over the soy sauce and honey and shake the pan to mix.

Pour in a good splash
of hot water and add the lemon slices. Let the liquid bubble and reduce down until syrupy, which will take about 10 minutes or so. By now the chicken should be cooked through.

Transfer the chicken
to a platter and sprinkle over the chopped parsley. Serve with the champ and green beans or steamed sugar snap peas.

Champ

Cut the potatoes into similar-sized chunks and boil in salted water for about 10 minutes until tender when pierced with a small sharp knife. Drain well.

Mash the potatoes while still hot, using a potato ricer if you have one, then stir through the butter and chopped spring onions.

Pour the cream and milk into a saucepan and bring just to the boil. Take off the heat and gradually pour on to the potatoes, mixing well. If the mash is too thick, add a little extra milk. Season generously and serve.

Serves 4

1kg floury potatoes (eg King Edward), peeled
sea salt and black pepper
30g butter
bunch of spring onions (about 6–8), trimmed and chopped
100ml double cream
100ml whole milk, plus extra if needed

CARAMELISED BANANA SPLIT

" Make sure you use good quality ice cream here. For extra child appeal, provide bowls with little extras, such as chocolate sprinkles and chocolate chips, so the kids can help themselves. **"**

Serves 4

4 ripe bananas

8 tbsp caster sugar

2–3 scoops each of different ice creams (eg vanilla, chocolate, strawberry)

150ml double cream, lightly whipped

sweetened dessicated coconut, to sprinkle (optional)

4 glacé (or pitted fresh) cherries

CHOCOLATE SAUCE:

100g dark chocolate, broken into pieces

2 tbsp runny honey

75ml double cream

Peel the bananas and cut in half lengthways.

Place cut side up on a sturdy baking tray and sprinkle evenly with the sugar. If you have a cook's blowtorch, wave it over the bananas until the sugar has caramelised. (Otherwise, preheat the grill to its highest setting and flash the bananas under the grill until golden brown and bubbling). Leave to cool until the sugar has firmed up.

Make the chocolate sauce in the

meantime. Put all the ingredients in a bowl set over a pan of simmering water and stir occasionally until the chocolate has melted and the sauce is smooth. Take the bowl off the pan and leave to cool.

Arrange two banana halves on

clear serving dishes (ideally oval or oblong), with the caramelised sides facing outwards. Place a scoop of each flavoured ice cream between the banana halves. Drizzle with chocolate sauce, then spoon or pipe over the whipped cream. Sprinkle with the coconut if using and top each banana split with a cherry. Serve immediately.

fish

Tandoori spiced halibut with cucumber
John Dory with sweet onions & kale
Lemon sole with caper mayonnaise
Sea trout with fennel & watercress
Brill with creamed cabbage & bacon

Tandoori spiced halibut with cucumber

Serves 4

4 skinned halibut fillets, about 150g each
1 tbsp tandoori or hot Madras curry paste
1 tbsp olive oil
1 tsp caster sugar
150g tub natural yogurt
2 cucumbers, peeled
handful of mint leaves, chopped
squeeze of lime juice
1–2 tbsp vegetable oil

Heat the oven to 200°C/Gas 6. Lay the halibut fillets on a plate. Mix the curry paste with the olive oil and sugar. Stir in all but 3 tbsp of the yogurt. Coat the fish with the spiced yogurt and set aside.

Cut the cucumbers lengthways using a swivel vegetable peeler into long wide strips, avoiding the seeds in the middle. Toss with the reserved 3 tbsp yogurt, chopped mint and lime juice.

Heat an ovenproof pan and add the vegetable oil. Scrape off the excess marinade from the halibut fillets and place them in the hot pan, reserving the marinade. Sear for 1–1½ minutes on each side until golden brown.

Spoon the marinade over the fish and place the pan in the oven for a few minutes to finish cooking. Transfer to warm plates, drizzle over the pan juices and serve with the cucumber salad.

John Dory with sweet onions & kale

Serves 4

400g kale, stalks removed, roughly
  shredded
sea salt and black pepper
4 tbsp olive oil
2 large onions, peeled and sliced
2 tsp caster sugar
knob of butter
2 tbsp sherry vinegar
4 John Dory fillets, about 175g each,
  skinned
50ml fish or chicken stock

Add the kale to a pan of boiling salted water and blanch for 3–4 minutes. Drain in a colander, refresh under cold running water and set aside.

Heat a sauté pan and add half the olive oil. Toss in the onions, season and sprinkle with the sugar. Add a splash of water and cook over a medium-high heat, stirring from time to time, for about 8 minutes until the onions are caramelised.

Add the blanched kale and a knob of butter. Toss well over the heat, then pour in the sherry vinegar and let bubble until it has reduced away.

Heat a large frying pan with the remaining oil. Season the fish fillets and fry for 2–2½ minutes until the fish is cooked two-thirds of the way through. Turn over and add the stock. Cook for 30–40 seconds until the fish is just cooked.

Divide the onions and kale among four serving plates. Place the fish fillets on top and pour over the juices from the pan. Serve immediately.

Lemon sole with caper mayonnaise

Serves 4

4 small (or 2 large) lemon sole, scaled
  and gutted
olive oil, to drizzle
sea salt and black pepper
few thyme sprigs
1 lemon, quartered

CAPER MAYONNAISE:
200ml mayonnaise (see page 248)
1 gherkin, finely chopped
1 tbsp capers, drained and chopped
1 tbsp chopped flat leaf parsley
½ small garlic clove, peeled and crushed
squeeze of lemon juice

Heat the oven to 200°C/Gas 6. Score the lemon sole at intervals along their length. Lightly oil two large baking trays and sprinkle with salt and pepper. Scatter over a few sprigs of thyme.

Lay the fish on top and drizzle with more olive oil. Sprinkle the fish with salt, pepper and some thyme leaves. Roast for about 15–20 minutes, depending on the size of the fish. It is cooked when the thickest part of the flesh pulls away easily from the bone.

Mix the ingredients for the caper mayonnaise together in the meantime. Season with salt and pepper to taste and add a little more lemon juice or water if you prefer a thinner consistency.

Serve the sole whole (or filleted if you've cooked 2 large fish) with the caper mayonnaise and lemon wedges for squeezing over.

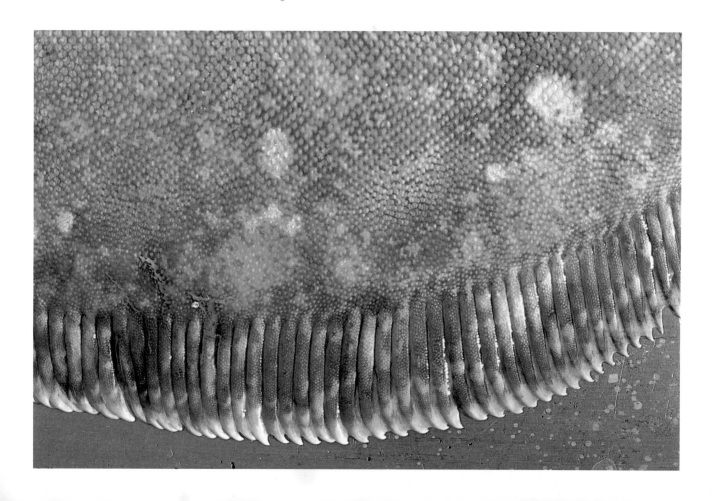

Sea trout with fennel & watercress

Serves 4

4 fennel bulbs, trimmed and tough outer
   leaves removed
1 tsp fennel seeds
sea salt and black pepper
5 tbsp olive oil, plus extra to drizzle
1½ tsp caster sugar
1 tbsp sherry vinegar
4 sea trout fillets, with skin, about
   150g each
bunch of watercress, about 100g, well
   washed and stems removed

Slice the fennel bulbs thinly. Crush the fennel seeds with a little salt using a pestle and mortar. Heat 3 tbsp olive oil in a saucepan and add the sliced fennel and crushed fennel seeds. Sprinkle over the sugar and cook over a high heat for 10 minutes, stirring well. Add the sherry vinegar and cook for another 5 minutes until the fennel is soft and caramelised.

Score the skin of the sea trout fillets at close intervals with a sharp knife. Heat the remaining oil in a wide sauté pan. Season the fish and fry, skin side down, until cooked two-thirds of the way through. Flip over and cook on the other side for 30 seconds.

Divide the fennel among four plates and sit the fish fillets on top. Garnish with watercress, drizzle with olive oil and serve.

Brill with creamed cabbage & bacon

Serves 4

4 tbsp olive oil

6 rashers of unsmoked streaky bacon,
  derinded and chopped

1 large carrot, peeled and diced

½ celeriac, peeled and diced

½ Savoy cabbage, cored and finely
  shredded

200ml double cream

sea salt and black pepper

4 brill fillets, about 150g each, skinned

large knob of butter

juice of ½ lemon

large handful of flat leaf parsley, chopped

Heat 2 tbsp olive oil in a large pan. Add the chopped bacon and fry for a few minutes, then stir in the carrot and celeriac. Cover the pan with a tight-fitting lid and cook for 8–10 minutes over a medium heat until the celeriac turns translucent.

Add the shredded cabbage and cook for 3–4 minutes, then pour in the cream. Simmer for a few minutes until the cream has thickened and the cabbage is tender. Season well and keep warm.

Meanwhile, heat a sauté pan and add the remaining olive oil. Season the fish with salt and pepper. When the pan is hot, add the fish, skinned side down, and fry for 1½ minutes until golden brown on the underside.

Flip the fish over and add the butter to the pan. Squeeze over the lemon juice and let bubble gently for 1–2 minutes. Toss in the parsley and spoon the herby butter over the fish. Take off the heat.

Spoon the creamed cabbage into the middle of four warm plates and top with the brill fillets. Spoon any remaining pan juices over the fish and serve.

Summer special

I love the simplicity of this menu. Full of summery flavours, it kicks off with a refreshing chilled soup, followed by tasty baked salmon fillets and a colourful tomato salad. Serve a cold glass of Vin Santo with the roasted nectarines for a perfect finish. Serves 4.

planning your menu

Avocado & cucumber soup

Salmon with Mediterranean flavours
+ Mixed tomato salad

Roasted nectarines with amaretti cream

- Make the soup and chill.
- Preheat the oven and stud the salmon with the flavourings.
- Prepare the tomato salad and dressing.
- Halve and stone the nectarines. Crush the amaretti.
- Put the salmon in the oven to bake.
- Prepare the amaretti cream and chill.
- When the salmon is ready, rest in a warm place while you serve the soup.
- Bake the nectarines.
- Dress the tomato salad and serve with the salmon.
- Plate the nectarines and amaretti cream to serve.

AVOCADO & CUCUMBER SOUP

"Use really ripe avocados to give this soup a rich green colour. If you want to take it a step further, add some cooked lobster or flaky crabmeat, or perhaps one or two Dublin Bay prawns, to the garnish. The perfect cooling starter, this soup can also be served as a light summer lunch with a crusty baguette."

Serves 4

2 large cucumbers, about 400g each, chilled

juice of 1 lemon, or to taste

2 ripe avocados

2 tbsp Greek yogurt

1 tbsp Worcestershire sauce

sea salt and black pepper

½ red onion, finely chopped

1 plum tomato, deseeded and finely chopped

1 tbsp olive oil, plus extra to drizzle

3–4 basil leaves, finely shredded

Peel the cucumbers,
quarter lengthways and remove the seeds. Dice a quarter and set aside for the garnish. Roughly chop the rest, place in a blender with half the lemon juice and whiz until smooth.

Halve, stone and peel
the avocados. Finely chop one avocado half to use for the garnish. Squeeze over a little lemon juice and set aside with the diced cucumber. Tip the rest of the avocados into the blender.

Blend the avocados
with the puréed cucumber, Greek yogurt and Worcestershire sauce until very smooth. Season generously with salt and pepper, and add lemon juice to taste. Chill until ready to serve.

For the garnish,
combine the diced cucumber and avocado with the red onion and tomato. Toss with the olive oil and shredded basil.

Taste the chilled soup
for seasoning and add a splash of cold water if it is too thick. Pour into four chilled bowls and spoon the garnish into the centre. Add a drizzle of olive oil and grind over a little pepper to serve.

SALMON WITH MEDITERRANEAN FLAVOURS

"Studding salmon fillets with little 'cloutes' of sun-dried tomato, basil, olive and garlic imparts some strong flavours and gives the fish a different character."

Serves 4

4 skinned salmon fillets, about 200g each

50g sun-dried tomatoes in oil, halved if large

handful of basil leaves

50g pitted black olives

3 large garlic cloves, peeled and thinly sliced

sea salt and black pepper

olive oil, to drizzle

Heat the oven to 200°C/Gas 6. Place the salmon fillets on a board, skinned side down. Use an apple corer to make 6 small holes in each fillet.

Flatten the sun-dried tomatoes and place a basil leaf, an olive and a sliver of garlic on each one. Roll up and use to stuff the holes in the salmon. Season with salt and pepper.

Place the salmon fillets on a lightly oiled baking tray. Drizzle with olive oil and bake for 6–8 minutes until medium-rare – the thickest part will feel slightly springy when pressed. Transfer to warm plates and serve with the tomato salad and country bread.

Mixed tomato salad

Halve larger tomatoes or cut into quarters; keep smaller ones whole. Place in a large serving bowl.

For the dressing, whisk the mustard, wine vinegar, sugar and olive oil together and season with salt and pepper to taste. (Or shake to combine in a screw-topped jar.)

Drizzle the dressing over the tomatoes and toss gently. Scatter the torn basil over the salad to serve.

Serves 4

600g mixed vine-ripened tomatoes (eg red and yellow cherry, plum, romano, green zebra)

handful of basil leaves, torn

DRESSING:

1 tsp Dijon mustard

1 tbsp red wine vinegar

½ tsp caster sugar

4 tbsp extra virgin olive oil

sea salt and black pepper

ROASTED NECTARINES
WITH AMARETTI CREAM

66 This works equally well with peaches – just make sure you use ripe, firm, juicy fruit. Immature nectarines or peaches would simply disappoint. **99**

Serves 4
4 ripe nectarines
a little oil, to oil
3–4 tbsp icing sugar
few knobs of butter
150ml double cream
250g mascarpone
1 tbsp amaretto liqueur (or milk)
50g amaretti biscuits, lightly crushed

Heat the oven to 200°C/Gas 6. Halve the nectarines, prise out the stones, then place cut side up on a lightly oiled baking sheet.

Dust the nectarines with the icing sugar and top each one with a knob of butter. Bake for 10–12 minutes or until the sugar topping has slightly caramelised. Place two nectarine halves on each shallow serving bowl and leave to cool slightly.

For the amaretti cream, whip the cream until soft peaks form. In another bowl, stir the mascarpone with the amaretto (or milk) to lighten it, then fold through the softly whipped cream. Fold through two-thirds of the crushed biscuits.

Top the baked nectarines with the amaretti cream and sprinkle over the remaining crushed biscuits. Serve at once.

Fast ways to cook meat

Buy tender cuts, apply suitable cooking techniques and tasty meat dishes can be on the table in no time:

Stir-frying Invest in a large, traditional wok (unless you already have one). Use tender cuts, like chicken breasts, beef fillet or rump, pork tenderloin and lamb fillet. Cut the meat (and flavouring vegetables) into small strips to ensure fast, even cooking and have everything ready before you start. Heat the wok over a high heat, add the oil, then get stir-frying.

Fast roasting Tender joints of meat such as rack of lamb, pork tenderloin and beef fillet can be roasted at a high temperature and take little time to cook. The meat should be trimmed or shaped to an even thickness to ensure even cooking and it must be rested after roasting – for at least 15 minutes.

Griddling and grilling Using intense heat, these methods produce succulent meat – brown and crisp on the outside and juicy within. Buy tender cuts – no thicker then 5cm, otherwise the meat will be charred on the outside before it is cooked in the centre. Preheat the grill or griddle to high and don't leave the meat unattended while it's cooking.

Pan-frying Chops, steaks and chicken breasts lend themselves to pan-frying in a little olive oil and/or butter. You'll need a large, wide heavy-based frying pan – avoid overcrowding otherwise the meat will stew rather than fry. Get the pan hot before you add the meat, but be ready to adjust the heat during cooking. Again, let the meat rest after cooking and do deglaze the pan with a little wine, stock or other liquor to retain all the tasty caramelised meat juices.

fast 5 meat

Quail with kohlrabi & butternut squash
Barnsley chop with garlic & herb butter
Beef rib-eye with baby turnips in port
Veal escalope with sautéed vegetables
Venison with sweet & sour peppers

Quail with kohlrabi & butternut squash

Serves 4

8 oven-ready quails, legs removed
  (leaving the crown and wing tips)
sea salt and black pepper
2 tbsp olive oil, plus extra to drizzle
30g butter, cut into cubes
few thyme sprigs
1 butternut squash, 700–800g, peeled,
  deseeded and cut into 2cm cubes
1 kohlrabi, about 400g, peeled and cut
  into 2cm cubes

Heat the oven to 200°C/Gas 6 and put a large roasting tray inside to heat up.

Season the quails and sear in a hot heavy-based pan with the olive oil over a high heat until golden brown all over (you may need to do this in two batches). Add the butter and thyme, spooning the butter into the quail cavities as it melts. Transfer the birds to a plate.

Toss the squash and kohlrabi into the pan. Season well and cook over a high heat for 2–3 minutes. Tip them into the hot roasting tray and sit the quails on top. Cook in the oven for 10 minutes. Lift the quails on to a warm platter and rest for 5 minutes. Return the vegetables to the oven for another 5 minutes or until they are tender.

To serve, divide the roasted vegetables among warm plates and place two quails on top. Drizzle with a little olive oil and serve.

Barnsley chop with garlic & herb butter

3 tbsp olive oil
4 Barnsley chops, about 350g each and
  4cm thick
few thyme sprigs

GARLIC AND HERB BUTTER:
60g unsalted butter, softened
1 fat garlic clove, peeled and finely
  crushed
handful of flat leaf parsley, chopped
small handful of mint, chopped
sea salt and black pepper

For the garlic and herb butter,
blend the softened butter with the garlic, chopped herbs and some seasoning. Spoon on to a piece of cling film and shape into a neat roll, wrapping the butter in the cling film and twisting the ends to seal. Pop into the freezer to chill while you prepare the chops (or in the fridge for at least 30 minutes if preparing ahead).

Heat the olive oil
in a large frying pan. (You may need to use two pans.) Season the chops with salt and pepper, then lift into the pan and add the thyme sprigs. Fry for 2½–3 minutes on each side, spooning the pan juices over the chops as they cook. The chops are ready when the meat feels slightly springy if lightly pressed.

Transfer the chops
to a warm platter and rest for a few minutes. Unwrap the garlic and herb butter and cut into 4 thick slices. Place a slice on top of each chop. The warmth of the chops will soon melt the butter, so serve them quickly.

Beef rib-eye with baby turnips in port

Serves 4

5 tbsp olive oil
400g baby turnips, washed and trimmed
few thyme sprigs
sea salt and black pepper
1 tsp Chinese five-spice powder
few knobs of butter
200ml port
1 tsp soft brown sugar
4 boneless rib-eye of beef steaks, about
  250g each and 3cm thick, trimmed

Heat 3 tbsp olive oil in a heavy-based pan and add the turnips, thyme and seasoning. Sauté for a minute, then add the five-spice and a couple of knobs of butter. Cook, tossing occasionally, for 8–10 minutes until golden brown.

Pour in the port, standing well back as it may flambé. Sprinkle in the sugar, stirring to dissolve, then let bubble for about 5 minutes until the liquor is reduced and syrupy.

Season the beef and sear in a hot ovenproof pan with the remaining oil. Fry for 3–4 minutes on each side, adding a knob of butter to finish off the cooking. For medium rare beef, the meat should be slightly springy when pressed. Rest the steaks in a warm place for 5 minutes before serving, with the glazed turnips.

Veal escalope with sautéed vegetables

Serves 4

4 British rose veal escalope, about 170g each and ½ cm thick
4 tbsp plain flour
3 tbsp olive oil

SAUTÉED VEGETABLES:
1 red pepper, cored and deseeded
1 yellow pepper, cored and deseeded
1 medium aubergine, trimmed
1 courgette, trimmed
4 tbsp olive oil
1 garlic clove (unpeeled), smashed
few thyme sprigs
sea salt and black pepper
splash of balsamic vinegar

Finely chop the vegetables. Heat 3 tbsp olive oil in a large frying pan with the garlic. Tip in the peppers, aubergine and thyme, and fry over a high heat for 3–4 minutes. Add the courgette.

Season and sauté for 2 minutes until the vegetables are just tender. Take off the heat and dress with the remaining olive oil and balsamic vinegar; check the seasoning. Keep warm.

Coat the veal all over with the flour seasoned with salt and pepper, shaking off any excess. Heat the olive oil in a wide pan and fry the veal over a high heat for 1½ minutes on each side until golden brown. (Do this in two batches if your pan is not wide enough.)

Transfer the escalopes to warm plates and spoon the sautéed vegetables over them to serve.

Venison with sweet & sour peppers

Serves 4

4 venison loin steaks, about 170g each
and 3cm thick
6–7 tbsp olive oil, plus extra to drizzle
sea salt and black pepper
1 tbsp juniper berries, lightly crushed
handful of thyme sprigs
3 red peppers, cored, deseeded and
sliced
3 yellow peppers, cored, deseeded
and sliced
2 tbsp white wine vinegar

TIP If you've had time to plan
ahead, marinate the venison with the
olive oil, juniper berries and thyme
overnight to help tenderise the meat.

Place the venison in a shallow dish and drizzle with 2–3 tbsp olive oil. Season lightly and scatter over the juniper berries and a few thyme sprigs. Leave to marinate while you cook the peppers.

Heat 2 tbsp olive oil in a large pan and add the red and yellow peppers with a little seasoning. Add a few thyme sprigs and cook over a medium heat for about 5 minutes. Pour in the wine vinegar and let bubble until the liquid has reduced right down. Remove from the heat and keep warm.

Season the venison with salt and pepper. Heat another heavy-based pan, then add the remaining olive oil. When it is very hot, sear the venison fillets for 3–4 minutes on each side. Leave to rest in a warm place for 5 minutes.

Divide the peppers among warm plates. Slice the venison fillets thickly on the diagonal and arrange on top of the peppers. Drizzle with a little olive oil to serve.

Indian spice
{everyday menu}

Based on the fragrant spices of southern Indian cooking, this pilau has a wonderful flavour, without the sweat-inducing kick of a fiery curry. Of course, you can spice it up with a few chopped chillies if you like. Minty griddled pineapple is a refreshing finish. Serves 4.

planning your menu

Prawn pilau
Wilted spinach with mustard seeds
Griddled pineapple with mint & toasted coconut

- Preheat the oven.
- Make the mint syrup and griddle the pineapple for the dessert; cool.
- Prepare the prawn pilau and put in the oven to cook.
- Skin and slice the pineapple, toss with the mint syrup and chill.
- Wash and drain the spinach; prepare the flavouring ingredients.
- Remove the pilau from oven and leave to stand for 5 minutes.
- Sauté the spinach.
- Serve the main course.
- Scatter mint and toasted coconut over the pineapple and serve.

PRAWN PILAU

"This mildly spiced Indian pilau is a terrific, easy one-pot supper. You can keep it simple and just use tiger prawns as suggested, or add other seafood such as sliced baby squid and/or firm fish like hake or halibut."

Serves 4

500ml light chicken stock
4 tbsp olive oil
1 large onion, peeled and finely chopped
1 garlic clove, peeled and chopped
1 tsp ground cumin
1 tsp ground coriander
1½ tsp mild curry powder
10 cardamom pods
few thyme sprigs (leaves only)
200g basmati rice
sea salt and black pepper
20 large tiger prawns (in shells)

Heat the oven to 200°C/Gas 6. Cut a circle of baking paper, big enough to generously cover a wide ovenproof pan. Cut a steam hole in the centre (fold the paper into segments, snip off the tip, then open out.) Bring the stock to the boil in another pan.

Heat the olive oil in the ovenproof pan and add the onion, garlic, spices and thyme. Stir over a medium heat for 2–3 minutes, then tip in the rice and stir well. Add some salt and pepper and toast the rice for a minute. Pour in the boiling stock and quickly arrange the prawns on top of the rice in a single layer.

Lay the baking paper on top to cover, then transfer the pan to the oven. Bake for 10–12 minutes or until the rice is just tender and has absorbed most of the liquid. Leave to stand, still covered with the paper, for 5 minutes before serving.

Wilted spinach with mustard seeds

Heat the oil in a large pan and fry the onion, garlic and ginger for 3–4 minutes until the onion begins to soften. Stir in the garam masala and mustard seeds and toast the spices for a minute until fragrant. (The mustard seeds may pop and jump out of the pan when heated; if so, cover with a lid for a few seconds.)

Throw in the spinach leaves a large handful at a time and stir quickly until the leaves begin to wilt. Season with salt and pepper to taste and serve.

Serves 4

3 tbsp vegetable oil
1 large onion, peeled and finely sliced
1 garlic clove, peeled and finely grated
2cm knob of fresh ginger, peeled and finely grated
½ tsp garam masala
1 tsp brown (or black) mustard seeds
400g spinach leaves, washed
sea salt and black pepper

GRIDDLED PINEAPPLE
WITH MINT & TOASTED COCONUT

66 Griddling pineapple helps to draw out its natural sweetness, which is particularly useful if you find the fruit is slightly under-ripe when you cut into it. If you're thinking ahead, prepare this dessert the night before – to give the pineapple plenty of time to infuse with the mint syrup. 99

Serves 4
75g caster sugar
small bunch of mint, plus shredded mint leaves to finish
1 large ripe pineapple
30g desiccated coconut, toasted

Put the sugar in a pan, add 150ml water and stir over a low heat until the sugar has dissolved. Increase the heat and bring to the boil. Throw in the mint sprigs, turn off the heat and leave to infuse the syrup as it cools.

Cut the pineapple into 8 wedges and cut out the core. Heat a griddle (or barbecue). Add the pineapple and griddle for 2–3 minutes on each side until charred. Leave to cool slightly.

Cut away the skin from the pineapple, then slice the griddled flesh thinly and place in a bowl. Take out the mint sprigs, then pour the infused syrup over the pineapples. Chill until ready to serve.

Divide the pineapple among individual bowls and spoon over the syrup. Sprinkle with the shredded mint leaves and toasted coconut to serve.

5 side dishes

Couscous, broad beans, peas & pancetta
Mixed vegetable stir-fry
Crunchy broccoli & cauliflower gratin
Sautéed potatoes with panch phora
Spicy fried rice with spring onions

Couscous, broad beans, peas & pancetta
Serves 4

Fry 250g chopped pancetta in a little olive oil until crisp. Remove with a slotted spoon and drain; save the oil in the pan.

Tip 250g couscous into a bowl and pour on 400ml hot chicken or vegetable stock. Add a squeeze of lemon juice and the reserved oil. Give the mixture a stir and cover the bowl tightly with cling film. Leave the couscous to absorb the liquid for 5–8 minutes.

Meanwhile, blanch 150g broad beans and 150g peas in boiling water for 2 minutes. Refresh under cold water and drain well.

Fluff up the couscous with a fork. Add the pancetta, beans, peas and a handful of chopped mint and flat leaf parsley. Season and drizzle generously with olive oil. Fork through and serve.

Mixed vegetable stir-fry

Serves 4

Slice 2 carrots, 2 celery stalks and ½ each sliced red, yellow and green pepper, keeping them separate.

Heat a wok until very hot, then add 2 tbsp each vegetable and sesame oil. Add 1 chopped garlic clove and the sliced carrots and stir-fry for 30 seconds.

Toss in the sliced peppers and stir-fry for another 30 seconds, then add the sliced celery and 200g bean sprouts and toss over the heat for another 30 seconds.

Add 1 tbsp dark soy sauce and 3 tbsp oyster sauce and mix well. Scatter with toasted sesame seeds and serve.

Crunchy broccoli & cauliflower gratin

Serves 4

Heat the oven to 220°C/Gas 7. Cut a small cauliflower and a head of broccoli into florets. Add the cauliflower to a large pan of boiling salted water and blanch for 1 minute. Tip in the broccoli and cook for another 2 minutes. Drain well and tip into a bowl.

Beat 200ml crème fraîche with 2 large egg yolks and some salt and pepper. Pour over the vegetables and toss well, then tip into an oiled large gratin dish.

Scatter over 50g lightly crushed toasted hazelnuts and top with a generous grating of Parmesan. Bake for 10 minutes or until the topping is golden brown. For a crisp topping, flash under a hot grill for a few minutes before serving.

Sautéed potatoes with panch phora

Peel 6 medium potatoes (eg King Edward or Maris Piper) and cut into 1cm thick slices. Add to a pan of boiling salted water and boil for 6 minutes until just tender. Drain well and pat dry between sheets of kitchen paper.

Heat 2 tbsp olive oil in a large sauté pan over a high heat. Add the potato slices and season with salt and pepper. Fry for about 3 minutes on each side until lightly golden.

Sprinkle with 1 tbsp panch phora spice mix and add a knob of butter to the pan. Sauté for 1–2 minutes, tossing and turning the potatoes in the spices, until golden brown and crisp at the edges. Serve immediately.

TIP Panch phora is a blend of five spices: brown mustard seeds, nigella seeds, fenugreek, cumin and fennel. If you can't find it, use ½ tsp of each spice for this dish.

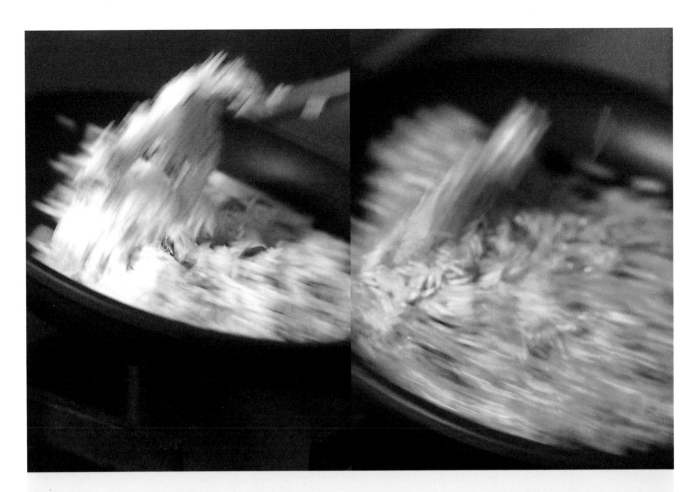

Spicy fried rice with spring onions

Serves 4

Heat a wok until very hot, then add 2 tbsp vegetable oil and 1 tbsp sesame oil. Throw in 1 tsp freshly grated ginger and 1 chopped garlic clove, and stir-fry for a minute until fragrant.

Toss in 600g cooked basmati (or jasmine) rice along with 5 or 6 chopped spring onions. Add a generous splash of dark soy sauce and 2–3 tbsp sweet chilli sauce. Stir-fry for a couple of minutes until the rice is piping hot. Drizzle with a little more sesame oil to taste, then serve.

TIP For an extra spicy and fiery kick, stir in 1 tsp sambal oelek, a south-east Asian spice paste, with the rice.

Thai feast
{entertaining menu}

I think of this as a celebration of Thai food – each dish highlighting the balance of sweet, sour, salty and hot flavours that are typical of the cuisine. It's worth trying to get hold of the authentic ingredients, especially if you have access to a good Asian grocery store, though I have suggested alternatives for the more unusual ingredients. Serves 4.

planning your menu

Yam pak salad
Thai red lobster curry
      + steamed jasmine rice
      + Chinese greens with shiitake mushrooms
Lychees with mint sugar

- Make the dressing for the salad and leave to cool.
- Peel the lychees and chill. Make the mint sugar.
- Cook the rice and make the curry (but don't add the lobster yet).
- Prepare the salad ingredients, toss with the dressing and serve.
- Add the lobster to the curry to warm through.
- Stir-fry the Chinese greens with shiitake mushrooms.
- Serve the lobster curry with rice and the Chinese greens.
- Serve the lychees with mint sugar.

YAM PAK SALAD

"I adore the combination of flavours in this fruity salad, which is perfectly complemented by the tamarind dressing. If you can't find Asian pears, substitute crisp green or red apples. For an authentic finish and extra crunch, I finish with a sprinkling of crispy fried shallots, which you can buy in small tubs from Oriental food stores. Use chopped, roasted peanuts, if you prefer."

Serves 4
1 large green or under-ripe mango
2 Asian pears
1 star fruit, trimmed
1 banana shallot, peeled and sliced into rings
large bunch of sweet Thai basil (leaves only), shredded
large bunch of mint (leaves only), shredded
2–3 tbsp crispy fried shallots (optional)

DRESSING:
1 tbsp tamarind paste
2 tbsp Thai fish sauce
2 tbsp palm (or soft dark brown) sugar
2 tbsp lime juice
2 tbsp sesame oil

TIP If using packed tamarind with seeds, put 25g in a small bowl and pour on a little boiling water. Stir to break it up into small pieces and leave to soak for 10 minutes. Push through a fine sieve to remove the seeds and use the strained juice.

First make the dressing. Put all the ingredients into a pan and stir over a medium heat until the sugar has dissolved and the dressing is smooth. Take off the heat and leave to cool completely.

Peel the mango and thinly slice the flesh away from the stone. Quarter, core and thinly slice the Asian pears. Thinly slice the star fruit.

Place the fruit, shallot rings and herbs in a large bowl, drizzle over the cooled dressing and toss gently to mix.

Pile the salad on to individual plates and garnish with a sprinkling of crispy shallots if you like, to serve.

THAI RED LOBSTER CURRY

" Nothing beats a good Thai curry and this one is so easy. The lobster tastes divine, but you can use monkfish, or strips of chicken, lamb or beef fillet – adding them at the start with the curry paste. If you can't get pea aubergines (available from Oriental food stores), use a regular aubergine or button mushrooms instead. "

Serves 4
2 tbsp vegetable oil
3 tbsp red curry paste
400ml coconut milk
1 tbsp Thai fish sauce
4–5 kaffir lime leaves
200g pea aubergines, stalks removed
4 cooked lobster tails, shelled
200g canned bamboo shoots, drained
sea salt and black pepper
1 tsp caster sugar (or palm sugar)
squeeze of lime juice

Heat a large saucepan
and add the oil, followed by the curry paste. Fry over a medium heat, stirring continuously, for 2 minutes until the paste is fragrant. Add the coconut milk, fish sauce and lime leaves and bring to the boil.

Add the pea aubergines
and cook for 5 minutes. Meanwhile, slice the lobster tails into large bite-sized pieces.

Add the bamboo shoots
to the curry and simmer for a couple of minutes. Tip in the lobster pieces and warm through briefly. Season with salt and pepper, and add the sugar and lime juice to taste. Serve at once, with rice.

Chinese greens with shiitake mushrooms

Trim the Chinese greens
and broccoli and halve the stems if they are too long to fit in a wok.

Heat a large wok
and add the oils. Tip in the shallot and mushrooms and stir-fry for 2 minutes. Add the garlic and stir-fry for another minute.

Toss in the greens
and broccoli, then add the soy and oyster sauces with a splash of water. Bring to the boil and keep tossing and turning over the heat for a couple of minutes until the greens are just tender. Drizzle over a little more sesame oil and transfer to a warm platter to serve.

Serves 4
400g Chinese greens (eg Chinese broccoli or bok choy)
200g tender stem broccoli
2 tbsp vegetable oil
1 tbsp sesame oil, plus extra to drizzle
1 banana shallot, peeled and thinly sliced
200g shiitake mushrooms, stalks removed and sliced
1 large garlic clove, peeled and thinly sliced
2 tbsp dark soy sauce
3 tbsp oyster sauce

LYCHEES WITH MINT SUGAR

“ If you are short of time, simply put a large bowl of lychees on the table and provide each guest with a small dipping bowl of mint sugar. Everyone can help themselves and peel their own lychees at their leisure. ”

Serves 4
500g fresh lychees
50g granulated sugar
pinch of sea salt
small bunch of mint, leaves only

Peel the lychees and divide among individual serving bowls.

Put the sugar, salt and mint leaves in a food processor and pulse for a few seconds only, until the mixture turns bright green. Do not over-process or the mint will turn black.

Spoon the mint sugar into four small dipping bowls to serve with the lychees.

fast 5 fruity desserts

Pain perdu with raspberries & ricotta
Mango fool
Cherries with almonds & mint
Figs & blackberries poached in red wine
Berry & Champagne soup

Pain perdu with raspberries & ricotta

Serves 4

125g ricotta cheese, drained
125g mascarpone
2 tbsp caster sugar
squeeze of lemon juice
200g raspberries
25g unsalted butter
4 slices raisin bread
3 large eggs, beaten
few basil sprigs, to finish
icing sugar, to sprinkle

Beat the ricotta, mascarpone, sugar and lemon juice together in a bowl, then gently fold through half of the raspberries to get a rippled effect.

Melt the butter in a wide, non-stick frying pan until it begins to foam. Dip the raisin bread into the beaten eggs, add to the pan and fry for a minute or two on each side until golden brown. Place each slice on a serving plate.

Spoon the ricotta mixture on to the warm pain perdu and tumble the remaining raspberries on top. Finish with basil sprigs and a sprinkling of icing sugar to serve.

Mango fool

Serves 4

1 large ripe mango
1–2 tbsp caster sugar (optional)
300ml double cream

Peel the mango and carefully cut the flesh away from the stone. Cut a quarter into neat, thin slices and set aside. Chop the rest into rough chunks.

Whiz the chunks of mango to a smooth purée in a blender or food processor, adding sugar to taste. (You may not need any if the mango is perfectly ripe.)

Whip the cream until soft peaks form, then lightly fold in three-quarters of the mango purée.

Divide the fool among serving glasses and spoon the remaining mango purée on top. Decorate each serving with a few slices of mango.

Cherries with almonds & mint

Serves 4

500g ripe cherries, pitted
1–2 tbsp caster sugar
splash of amaretto liqueur
squeeze of lemon juice
50g flaked almonds, toasted
small handful of mint leaves, chopped
clotted cream or crème fraîche, to serve

Warm the cherries and sugar in a non-stick pan until the sugar begins to dissolve and the cherries start to release their juices. Add the amaretto and lemon juice and cook for a few more minutes until the liquid has reduced down.

Divide the cherries among small serving bowls and scatter over the toasted almonds and chopped mint.

Serve topped with a generous dollop of clotted cream or crème fraîche.

Figs & blackberries poached in red wine
Serves 4

1 vanilla pod
250ml red wine (eg a young Merlot)
1 cinnamon stick
4 cloves
2 star anise
100g sugar
3 figs, cut into quarters
500g blackberries
250g mascarpone
2 tbsp icing sugar

Split the vanilla pod lengthways, scrape out the seeds with the back of the knife and reserve.

Put the wine, empty vanilla pod, cinnamon stick, cloves, star anise and sugar into a saucepan and slowly bring to the boil, stirring to dissolve the sugar. Lower the heat to a simmer, add the fruit and poach gently for 8–10 minutes. Allow to cool completely.

Put the mascarpone into a bowl and sift in the icing sugar. Add the reserved vanilla seeds and beat well.

Divide the poached fruit among four bowls and serve with the vanilla mascarpone.

Berry & Champagne soup

Serves 4

125g blackberries
125g blueberries
125g redcurrants
125g raspberries
handful of mint leaves
2–3 tbsp caster sugar
200ml natural yogurt
200ml double cream
300ml Champagne or sparkling wine,
   chilled

TIP A great way to use up the last of the
season's berries, particularly if you have some
over-ripe fruit in the fridge. Freeze them before
blending for a refreshing ice-cool dessert.

Tip all the berries into a blender and whiz to a
purée. Add the mint leaves and sugar to taste, and blitz until the mint is
finely chopped. Pour in the yogurt, cream and Champagne and whiz
until evenly blended and frothy.

Pour the soup into serving glasses or individual bowls
and serve immediately.

Speedy sunday lunch

{everyday menu}

I love a traditional roast, but sometimes there just isn't enough time. When the first warm sunny days appear in spring, Tana and I want to be outdoors with the kids making the most of them. This is the perfect menu – quick, easy and full of spring flavours – young tender lamb, fresh peas and tart gooseberries. Serves 4.

New season's lamb with crushed peas
+ minted new potatoes
Crunchy gooseberry crumble

planning your menu

- Preheat the oven.
- Prepare the gooseberries and divide among baking dishes.
- Prepare the crumble topping.
- Poach the lamb.
- Boil the new potatoes and blanch the fresh peas.
- Set the lamb aside to rest for 10 minutes.
- Assemble the crumble and bake.
- Blend the peas and warm through.
- Drain the potatoes and toss in butter with some chopped mint.
- Slice the lamb, plate with the crushed peas and serve with the potatoes.
- Remove crumble from oven and leave to stand for 5–10 minutes before serving.

NEW SEASON'S LAMB WITH CRUSHED PEAS

"People don't generally think of poaching lamb, but I find it's a really good way to cook this pink, delicate meat and ensure a succulent, flavourful result, particularly if you add lots of aromatics to the cooking liquor as I do."

Serves 4

4 rumps of new season's lamb, about 140g each, trimmed
800ml chicken stock
few thyme sprigs
1 bay leaf
1 tbsp black peppercorns
1 tbsp coriander seeds
300g fresh peas (or frozen and thawed)
generous drizzle of olive oil
2 tbsp chopped oregano, plus extra leaves to garnish
sea salt and black pepper
extra virgin olive oil, to drizzle

Place the lamb rumps in a cooking pot or heavy-based pan with the stock, thyme, bay leaf, peppercorns and coriander seeds. Bring just to the boil, then immediately turn down the heat and simmer for 8 minutes.

In the meantime, if using fresh peas, add to a pan of boiling water and blanch for 2–3 minutes, depending on size. Drain well. Tip the blanched (or thawed, frozen) peas into a food processor and pulse for a few seconds to crush slightly.

Remove the lamb from the poaching liquid to a warm plate and leave to rest for 10 minutes.

Tip the crushed peas into a pan and add a generous drizzle of olive oil, the chopped oregano and salt and pepper to taste. Warm through briefly over a medium heat, stirring frequently.

Spoon the peas on to warm serving plates (into a metal ring if you want to shape a neat circle). Slice the lamb into thick pieces and arrange on top. Scatter over a few oregano leaves and add a drizzle of extra virgin olive oil. Sprinkle with sea salt and coarsely ground black pepper to serve.

CRUNCHY GOOSEBERRY CRUMBLE

" Tart green gooseberries are ideal for a crumble, especially if you apply a sweet, crunchy oat topping. Gooseberries vary in acidity, so taste one before cooking to see whether you might need to adjust the amount of sugar in the recipe. "

Serves 4
450g gooseberries
75g caster sugar, or to taste

TOPPING:
175g crunchy oat cereal or granola
1 tbsp demerara sugar
25g slightly salted butter, cut into
**   small dice**

TIP Gooseberries have a relatively short season but they do freeze well and frozen gooseberries, defrosted at room temperature, are fine for this crumble. Or you can substitute chopped rhubarb, or a mixture of chopped apples and blackcurrants or blackberries.

Heat the oven to 200°C/Gas 6 and place a baking sheet inside to heat up. Wash the gooseberries, remove the husks and pat dry with a clean tea towel.

Tip the gooseberries into a pan, add the sugar and place over a high heat until they begin to release their juices, shaking the pan frequently. Divide the gooseberries among four individual ovenproof dishes.

For the topping, mix the crunchy cereal and demerara sugar together.

Sprinkle evenly over the gooseberries to cover them and dot with the butter. Bake for about 10–15 minutes until the topping is golden brown and the gooseberries are bubbling up around the sides. Leave to stand for 5–10 minutes to cool down slightly before serving.

226

*f*ast creamy desserts

Banana mousse with butterscotch ripple
White chocolate & cherry mousse
Chocolate fondant
Summer fruit trifles
Baked ricotta with caramelised peaches

Banana mousse with butterscotch ripple

Serves 4

100g light brown sugar
40g unsalted butter
550ml double cream, chilled
4 large ripe bananas, ideally chilled in
   the freezer for 1–2 hours
squeeze of lemon juice
dark chocolate, for grating

Put the sugar, butter and 150ml of the cream in a pan
over a medium heat and stir continuously until the sugar is dissolved
and the butter melted. Let bubble for a minute or two, stirring frequently,
then remove from the heat and leave the sauce to cool completely.

Pour the remaining cream into a blender.
Peel and chop the bananas and add to the blender along with a
squeeze of lemon juice. Whiz until smooth, thick and creamy.

Spoon a little sauce around the sides of four
glasses, smudging some of it for an attractive effect. Divide the banana
mousse among the glasses and top with more butterscotch. Use a
small teaspoon to ripple the butterscotch through the mousse. Grate
over a little dark chocolate and chill until ready to serve.

White chocolate & cherry mousse

Serves 4

50g caster sugar
50ml kirsch or brandy
½ cinnamon stick
100g ripe cherries, pitted
200g white chocolate
350ml double cream
dark chocolate, for grating

Put the sugar, kirsch, 50ml water and the cinnamon in a
small saucepan over a low heat until the sugar is dissolved, then bring
to the boil. Add the cherries and simmer for 3–4 minutes until they are
tender but still holding their shape. Leave to cool in the syrup.

Chop the white chocolate into small pieces
and tip into a large bowl. Heat a third of the cream in a saucepan until
just beginning to boil, then slowly pour on to the white chocolate,
stirring continuously. Keep stirring until all the chocolate has melted.
Set aside to cool.

Whip the remaining cream until thick, then
fold in the cooled chocolate mixture. Keep whisking to stiff peaks if the
combined mixture is not thick enough.

Drain the cherries and set aside four for decoration.
Divide the rest among individual glasses and pipe or spoon the white
chocolate mousse over them. Top each serving with a cherry and grate
over some dark chocolate to serve.

Chocolate fondant

Serves 4

50g unsalted butter, plus extra to grease
2 tsp cocoa powder, to dust
50g good quality dark, bitter chocolate
(minimum 70% cocoa solids), in pieces
1 large egg
1 large egg yolk
60g caster sugar
2 tbsp Tia Maria liqueur
50g plain flour, sifted
crème fraîche or vanilla ice cream,
to serve

Heat the oven to 160°C/Gas 3. Butter four ramekins (7.5cm in diameter) and dust liberally with cocoa powder. Melt the chocolate and butter in a small bowl set over a pan of hot water, then take off the heat and stir until smooth.

Using an electric whisk, beat the whole egg, egg yolk and sugar together until pale and thick, then incorporate the chocolate mixture. Fold in the liqueur, followed by the flour.

Divide the chocolate mixture among the ramekins and bake for 12 minutes. Turn the chocolate fondants out on to warm plates and serve immediately with a dollop of crème fraîche or a scoop of vanilla ice cream.

Summer fruit trifles

Serves 4

200g strawberries, hulled and quartered
600g other mixed berries (eg blueberries,
   blackberries, raspberries)
3 tbsp caster sugar
100g amaretti biscuits
600ml good quality ready-made vanilla
   custard, chilled

Put the berries and sugar in a non-stick pan and heat gently for a few minutes until the fruit begins to soften. Transfer to a bowl and leave to cool completely. Using a slotted spoon, remove a spoonful of fruit for the topping and set aside.

Place the amaretti biscuits in a deep bowl and lightly crush with the end of a rolling pin. Reserving a handful, tip the rest into a large glass bowl (or divide among individual glasses).

Spoon half the custard over the amaretti, followed by half of the fruit compote. Repeat these layers and top with a sprinkling of crushed amaretti and the reserved fruit to serve.

233

Baked ricotta with caramelised peaches

Serves 4

25g butter, plus extra (softened), to grease
85g icing sugar, plus 2 tbsp to dust
500g ricotta cheese, drained
2 large eggs
finely grated zest and juice of 1 lemon
3–4 tbsp caster sugar, to dredge
4 ripe peaches, stoned and cut into wedges

Heat the oven to 200°C/Gas 6. Generously butter the base and sides of four ramekins, then dust with icing sugar, tilting the ramekins from side to side to ensure an even coating.

Mix the ricotta, eggs, lemon zest and icing sugar in a large bowl with a fork until evenly combined. Spoon into the ramekins and stand on a baking sheet. Bake for 15–20 minutes until golden brown around the edges and quite firm in the middle. Leave to cool.

Dredge the peach wedges in caster sugar. Fry in a non-stick frying pan with the remaining butter until caramelised. Add the lemon juice, shaking the pan to deglaze. Take off the heat.

Turn out the ricottas on to individual plates. Arrange the caramelised peaches around and spoon over any pan juices to serve.

My favourite time-saving tools

Having the right basic tools in the kitchen can make a big impact on speed and efficiency. A set of sharp knives is essential. Here are a few other time-saving items I can't do without:

Hand-blender A good professional model with a few variable operating speeds is vital for making velvety smooth soups, vegetable and fruit purées, and smoothies. I also use it to lighten sauces – blitzing directly in the pan means less washing up.

Cook's blowtorch This is brilliant for caramelising dessert toppings (crème brulée, for example) and it is quicker, more effective and easier to control than using the grill. Domestic versions are now relatively inexpensive and easy to find, so if you haven't got one already, treat yourself!

Mandolin No matter how good your knife skills, a mandolin is a handy tool to slice vegetables and fruits quickly and evenly. Although you can get them in wood or stainless steel, my favourite mandolin is a plastic Japanese version with a very sharp blade and a safety hand guard.

Microplane grater This costs more than a standard box grater but its razor-sharp blades will last for many years, saving you time and money in the long run. I use mine to zest citrus fruit and grate all kinds of ingredients, from garlic and ginger to hard cheeses and chocolate.

Food processor or mini-chopper I generally use my food processor to make pastry and crumble toppings but it is also useful for fast chopping vegetables, making curry pastes, even mincing meat.

fast drinks party
{entertaining menu}

We love having friends over for drinks and often find ourselves in the kitchen beforehand, hastily assembling finger foods to serve with Champagne, cocktails or wine. All of the nibbles on this menu are unbelievably easy and foolproof, but together they are infinitely more impressive than bowls of salty nuts and crisps. Serves 10.

planning your menu

Crispy Parma ham with asparagus
Cherry tomato & feta kebabs
Olives wrapped in anchovies
Smoked salmon & horseradish cream on pumperknickel
Minty mojito
Blueberry & pomegranate fizz

- Soften the blueberries and prise out the seeds from the pomegranate.
- Blanch and refresh the asparagus, then roll in the Parma ham.
- Make the tomato and feta kebabs. Wrap the olives in anchovies.
- Assemble the salmon and horseradish cream on pumperknickel.
- Make the minty mojito cocktail.
- Fry the wrapped asparagus spears and keep warm.
- Make the fizz and serve the drinks with the nibbles.

CRISPY PARMA HAM WITH ASPARAGUS

66 These asparagus rolls are sophisticated enough for a drinks party, but they are just as popular with children. Tana even puts them in the kid's lunchboxes. 99

Serves 10
30 asparagus spears, trimmed
sea salt and black pepper
15 slices Parma ham
3–4 tbsp olive oil

Blanch the asparagus in boiling salted water for 2–3 minutes until bright green and just tender. Drain and refresh under cold running water, then drain again and pat dry.

Cut each Parma ham slice in half lengthways and wrap around an asparagus spear.

Fry the asparagus rolls in a hot pan with a little olive oil, turning frequently, for 2–3 minutes until the ham is crisp. Grind over a little pepper and serve.

CHERRY TOMATO & FETA KEBABS

66 These are so easy you could get young children to make them. Try drizzling a little balsamic vinegar over the kebabs as you serve them. 99

Cut the feta into 2cm cubes and halve the cherry tomatoes. Thread them on to cocktail sticks, sandwiching a feta cube between two tomato halves. Thread a basil leaf on to each end and arrange the kebabs on a serving plate.

Just before serving, drizzle a little extra virgin olive oil over the kebabs and sprinkle with a little freshly ground pepper.

Serves 10
300g feta cheese
30 cherry tomatoes
30 small basil leaves
extra virgin olive oil, to drizzle
black pepper

OLIVES WRAPPED IN ANCHOVIES

“ Fresh marinated anchovies from the supermarket chiller cabinet are perfect for this nibble. Otherwise use good quality canned anchovy fillets in olive oil. ”

Serves 10

30 marinated anchovies or anchovy fillets in olive oil

30 Kalamata olives

Wrap an anchovy fillet around each
olive and secure with a cocktail stick. Arrange on a platter.

SMOKED SALMON
& HORSERADISH CREAM ON PUMPERNICKEL

“ Dark pumperknickel bread with its nutty flavour, sets off savoury smoked salmon and creamy horseradish to delicious effect. ”

Serves 10

120ml crème fraîche

2–3 tbsp creamed horseradish sauce

sea salt and black pepper

10 thin slices pumpernickel, toasted

400g smoked salmon slices

Mix the crème fraîche and
horseradish sauce together and season with salt and pepper to taste, then spread on top of each slice of toasted pumpernickel. Lay the smoked salmon slices on top and trim the edges to neaten. Cut into bite-sized pieces and arrange on a serving platter.

MINTY MOJITO

"This is one of my favourite drinks on holiday by the beach, and it's also fun to make at home. I tend to make my cocktails fairly strong, but you could always add more soda water... or less if you prefer."

Serves 10
plenty of crushed ice
150g caster sugar
6–8 limes, halved
1 large bunch of mint
250ml white or light rum
about 500ml soda water

Half-fill a large jug
with crushed ice and sprinkle in the sugar. Grate the zest from one of the limes into the jug, then squeeze the juice from all of the limes and add to the jug. Drop in the spent lime halves that haven't been zested.

Snip the leaves
from the bunch of mint into the jug and gently crush against the ice with a spoon.

Pour in the rum
and add soda water to taste. Stir well and pour into chilled glasses to serve.

BLUEBERRY & POMEGRANATE FIZZ

"I love this fruity champagne cocktail (illustrated on page 239). For a milder tipple, dilute the fizz with some blueberry and pomegranate juice. Spoon the blueberries and pomegranate seeds into each glass, one-third fill with the fruit juice and top up with Champagne."

Heat a frying pan
until hot, then tip in the blueberries and sugar and add a little splash of water. Place over a medium heat for a minute to slightly soften the berries. Tip on to a plate and leave to cool. Meanwhile, carefully prise out the seeds from the pomegranate avoiding the bitter membrane.

Put a spoonful of blueberries
and a sprinkling of pomegranate seeds into 10 champagne flutes. Pour over the chilled Champagne and serve at once.

Serves 10
150g blueberries
2 tsp caster sugar
1 pomegranate
1 bottle of Champagne, well chilled

BASICS

I appreciate the need to take shortcuts, but some convenience foods are strictly off limits – including awful-tasting stock cubes and almost all ready-made sauces in jars. A few basics are really worth the time and effort you spend making them.

A good example is mayonnaise. No commercial variety can ever compare to homemade mayonnaise, both in terms of flavour and consistency. Invariably, commercial mayonnaise is packed with sugar, preservatives and flavour enhancers – so you are also getting hit with lots of additives.

I'm often asked how the quality of good restaurant food can be replicated at home. I always say: start with the basics. Use good quality stocks and sauces and you are halfway to perfecting a dish. Whenever you have an hour or two to spare, make up a quantity of stock and freeze in smaller amounts, so you always have some to hand. If you run out and need to resort to ready-made alternatives, buy good quality fresh stock in cartons or jars. The other basic recipes here are quick and easy to make – keep in screw-topped jars in the fridge to use during the week.

Chicken stock • Fish stock • Vegetable stock
Classic vinaigrette • Mayonnaise • Pesto • Sweet chilli dipping sauce

Chicken stock

Makes about 1.5 litres

2 tbsp olive oil
1 carrot, peeled and chopped
1 onion, peeled and chopped
2 celery sticks, chopped
1 leek, washed and sliced
1 bay leaf
1 thyme sprig
3 garlic cloves, peeled
2 tbsp tomato purée
2 tbsp plain flour
1kg raw chicken bones
sea salt and black pepper

Heat the olive oil in a large stockpot and add the vegetables, herbs and garlic. Cook over a medium heat, stirring occasionally, until the vegetables are golden. Stir in the tomato purée and flour and cook for another minute. Add the chicken bones, then pour in enough cold water to cover. Season lightly. Bring to the boil and skim off any scum that rises to the surface. Reduce the heat and leave to simmer gently for 1 hour.

Let the stock stand for a few minutes (to cool slightly and allow the ingredients to settle) before passing through a fine sieve. Leave to cool. Refrigerate and use within 5 days, or freeze the stock in convenient portions for up to 3 months.

Brown chicken stock
Make as above, first roasting the chicken bones at 200°C/Gas 6 for 20 minutes. This stock lends a greater depth of flavour to a dish.

Fish stock

Makes about 1 litre

2 tbsp olive oil
1 small onion, peeled and chopped
½ celery stick, sliced
1 small fennel bulb, chopped
sea salt and black pepper
1kg white fish bones and trimmings
   (or crab or lobster shells)
75ml dry white wine

Heat the olive oil in a stockpot and add the onion, celery, fennel and a little salt and pepper. Stir over a medium heat for 3–4 minutes until the vegetables begin to soften but not brown. Add the fish bones and trimmings and pour in enough cold water to cover the ingredients. Simmer for 20 minutes, then remove the pan from the heat and leave to cool.

Ladle the stock through a fine sieve and discard the solids. Refrigerate and use within 2 days, or freeze in smaller quantities for up to 3 months.

Vegetable stock

Makes about 1.5 litres

3 onions, peeled and roughly
    chopped

1 leek, washed and roughly chopped

2 celery sticks, roughly chopped

6 carrots, peeled and roughly
    chopped

1 head of garlic, halved crossways

1 tsp white peppercorns

1 bay leaf

few thyme, basil, tarragon, coriander
    and parsley sprigs, tied together

200ml dry white wine

sea salt and black pepper

Put the vegetables, garlic, peppercorns and bay leaf in a large stockpot and pour on cold water to cover, about 2 litres. Bring to the boil, lower the heat to a simmer and leave to cook gently for 20 minutes. Remove the pan from the heat and add the bundle of herbs, white wine and a little seasoning. Give the stock a stir and leave to cool completely.

If you have time, chill the stock overnight before straining. Pass the liquid through a fine sieve. Refrigerate and use within 5 days, or freeze in smaller amounts for up to 3 months.

Classic vinaigrette

Makes about 250ml

100ml extra virgin olive oil

100ml groundnut oil

3 tbsp white wine vinegar

1 scant tsp Dijon mustard

sea salt and black pepper

Put the ingredients in a measuring jug and whisk together to emulsify (or use a stick blender to combine).

Pour into a clean squeezy bottle or screw-topped jar and seal. Keep in the fridge or cool larder for up to a week. Shake well before each use.

Mayonnaise

Makes about 300ml

2 large egg yolks

1 tsp white wine vinegar

1 tsp English or Dijon mustard

sea salt and white pepper

300ml groundnut oil

Put the egg yolks, wine vinegar, mustard and a pinch of salt in a food processor (fitted with a small bowl attachment, if you have one). Whiz for a few minutes until thick and creamy. With the motor running, slowly trickle in the groundnut oil in a thin stream until the mayonnaise is thick and emulsified. Season generously with salt and pepper.

Transfer the mayonnaise to a bowl or jar, cover and refrigerate. Use within 3 days.

note If the mayonnaise splits as you are adding the oil, transfer the mixture to a jug. Put another egg yolk, a little mustard and seasoning into the food processor and whiz for a minute or two, then slowly add the split mayonnaise. It should re-emulsify.

Pesto

Makes about 250ml

50g pine nuts

large bunch of basil, leaves picked

3 garlic cloves, peeled

50g Parmesan, freshly grated

125ml olive oil, plus extra to seal

sea salt and black pepper

Lightly toast the pine nuts in a dry frying pan over a medium heat, then tip on to a plate and leave to cool. Put the pine nuts, basil leaves, garlic and grated Parmesan in a blender or food processor and blitz to a rough paste. With the motor running, slowly pour in the olive oil through the funnel. You will need to stop the machine and scrape down the sides with a spatula a few times. When fully combined, season to taste with salt and pepper.

Transfer the pesto to a screw-topped jar, pour a thin layer of olive oil over the surface and cover with the lid. It will keep well in the fridge for up to a week, particularly if you re-cover the surface with a fresh layer of olive oil after each use.

Sweet chilli dipping sauce

Makes 200–250ml

100g caster sugar

5 garlic cloves, peeled

5cm piece fresh root ginger, peeled and roughly chopped

5–6 long red chillies, deseeded and roughly chopped

small handful of coriander leaves

juice of 2 large limes

2 tbsp light soy sauce

2 tbsp Thai fish sauce

Put the sugar in a small heavy-based saucepan with about 100ml water. Stir over a low heat to dissolve the sugar, then bring to the boil. Let bubble for 5–8 minutes to reduce and thicken. In the meantime, put the garlic, ginger, red chillies, coriander and lime juice in a food processor and pulse for a few seconds to a coarse paste.

When the sugar syrup has reached a light golden colour, carefully add the spice paste, standing back as the caramel will splutter and spit. Stir in the soy and fish sauces. Return to the boil, then immediately take the pan off the heat and leave to cool completely. Pour into a clean jar, refrigerate and use within a week.

INDEX

ACKNOWLEDGEMENTS

I owe my thanks to the talented, dedicated team who, once again, have worked so hard to produce this quality book: Mark Sargeant, Emily Quah, Jill Mead, Helen Lewis and Janet Illsley. I am especially grateful to Pat Llewellyn and everyone at Optomen TV for producing another great series, and to Anne Furniss and Alison Cathie of Quadrille, for publishing the book to accompany it. Also to Jo Barnes for her determination to make this book another huge success.

As ever, I'm truly appreciative of everyone at Gordon Ramsay Holdings, from Gillian Thomson to Chris Hutcheson. And last but not least, a big thank you to my wife Tana and our wonderful children: Megan, Jack, Holly and Tilly.

Editorial director **Anne Furniss**
Art director **Helen Lewis**
Project editor **Janet Illsley**
Photographer **Jill Mead**
Food stylist **Mark Sargeant**
Home economist **Emily Quah**
Assistant designer **Katherine Case**
Editorial assistant **Andrew Bayliss**
Production **Vincent Smith, Ruth Deary**

Optomen Television:
Managing director **Patricia Llewellyn**
Executive producer, F Word **Ben Adler**
Executive producer **Jon Swain**
Series editor **Deborah Sargeant**
Assistant producer **Lauren Abery**

Optomen Television Limited
1, Valentine Place
London SE1 8QH
www.optomen.com

optomen

This paperback edition first published in 2009 by
Quadrille Publishing Limited
Alhambra House, 27-31 Charing Cross Road, London WC2H 0LS
www.quadrille.co.uk

10 9 8 7 6 5 4 3 2 1

Text © 2007 Gordon Ramsay
Photography © 2007 Jill Mead
Design and layout © 2007 Quadrille Publishing Limited
Format and programme © 2007 Optomen Television Limited

The rights of the author have been asserted.

Cataloguing in Publication Data: a catalogue record for this book is available from the British Library.

ISBN 978 184400 761 5

Printed in Spain

The author would like to thank The Shop at Bluebird, London SW3 and Ted Baker for supplying clothes for photography.